LETTERS FROM THE KING

LETTERS FROM THE KING

A DEVOTIONAL PARABLE OF SPIRITUAL DISCOVERY FOR WORKING WOMEN

DANITA BYE

with My Father's Words and Meditations contributed by

PRISCILLA MOHRENWEISER

PUBLISHED BY

SGS, Inc.

Letters from the King ~ A Devotional Parable of Spiritual Discovery
for Working Women

Published by SGS, Inc.
Stanley, North Dakota

ISBN-13: 978-0-9845899-3-7

Design & Production by
Pettit Network Inc / Mark Griffin
and Wendy Holdman
Printed in China by
Pettit Network Inc.

To my children, Brittany, Westin, and Danae.
May you walk in the purpose, power, and presence
of our Most High King.

CONTENTS

WITH SPECIAL GRATITUDE TO...

My husband, Gordon, who faithfully supports and encourages me, even though I'm always picking more than two things to have on my plate.

My children, for being gracious to me, even when I had too many things on my to-do list . . . and for teaching me about God's love.

My parents, who are living a legacy of being faithful followers and mentoring the truth of Habakkuk 3:17-18, "Though the fig tree does not blossom and no fruit is on the vines . . . yet will I rejoice in the Lord."

Priscilla, you are a wonderful mentor. You live the truths that God speaks when we listen and that our highest calling is to love.

The numerous people who have mentored me in my faith walk through every worshipping community I've been involved with.

The Bethel Seminary professors, who demonstrated a power of strong intellect with critical thinking and gracious love and compassion.

David Monroy for his constant encouragement to "Pursue love, and earnestly desire the spiritual gifts, especially that you may prophesy" (1 Cor. 14:1 *ESV*).

THE KING'S CASTLE

My footsteps echoed as I walked through the castle toward my father's throne room. I loved the long halls with white marble pillars and rich silk tapestries in royal purple and blue. I reveled in the sparkling chandeliers and the grand guards at every soaring, vaulted doorway. This was the home I knew so well.

Today, however, as I walked the familiar route, I saw a pair of muddy, brown leather gloves on a hallway bench, perhaps left by staff. Seeing the mud, I was instantly transported to my unhappy past, to my life before being adopted into the royal family.

I had been a poor peasant child, from the notoriously corrupt village of Amuck. My mother was a barmaid, and not sure who my father was. I had two brothers, both older than me by quite a few years, who ran with a rough crowd and were forever in trouble with the law.

I passed my early childhood years virtually unnoticed and unsupervised by my family, and overlooked by the busy people around me. I tried to ignore my disheartening family situation, and passed the time playing in my grubby clothes on the bank of a small stream outside the village.

One morning, when I had reached the age of seven or so, the royal processional passed on the road near the stream in a tinkling of horse-harness chains and jouncing carriages. The wooden sides and doors on the conveyances had been polished until they sparkled, and even the golden paint on the wheel rims gleamed. What a display of finery and majesty! Though I had overheard others speak of the loveliness of these conveyances, I had never seen such a sight in all my young life.

Immediately, I left the place where I had been making mud balls and ran to get a closer look at the king's brigade. My eyes widened with surprise when the entire processional halted right in front of me! My shock increased, and then turned to fear, as a door opened and the king himself, resplendent, stepped out to meet me. Nervously, I wiped my dirty hands on my filthy dress.

"Hello, little one," he said to me, his eyes smiling with love. "How is the mud today?"

With those words, my fear of him melted away.

"It's real good." I smiled shyly, revealing the gap where my front teeth should have been. Recalling it, I pulled my lips together.

With great gentleness, the king lifted me in his arms, the mud smearing his fine purple robes, and held me for a long time.

I couldn't remember ever having felt this totally and completely loved. It was like he saw me clean and not muddy. Like he didn't notice my missing teeth or skinned elbows. It was as if he didn't see any of the bad in me, but saw only good, outside and in, and would always, only, see me that way.

I felt as though he was wrapping me in a golden blanket of love that he had hand-made just for me.

I rested my head on his shoulder.

Then worry, my constant companion, was suddenly gone. The fear that always haunted me that I would always feel defeated and alone without a hand to help lift me, was gone.

My shame at having never been good enough faded. The doubt that I would never become a worthy person, melted into nothingness.

He held me like a father who had been separated from his sole child long ago, and today had finally found her again.

In his arms, I knew that all was going to be okay from this day on.

MY FATHER'S WORDS

Though he spoke no words aloud as he held me, I heard his gentle voice within my thoughts, as though he were saying to me and everyone he loved, *"My beloved children, rejoice in spending time in my presence. Conversation and fellowship between an earthly father and his children can be exceedingly sweet. Conversation and fellowship between me and my children can be like heaven itself. I have not called you to be my servants. I have called you to be my family."*

As my awareness of the present moment returned, I glanced again at the pair of muddy gloves lying on the bench. The memories of my unhappy past faded. I was now the daughter of the king, and he the father of me. He had not only adopted me, I thought with a smile; I had happily embraced the wonderful king who had lifted me and held me while I was still covered in mud.

My eyes lifted to the two elegant, golden picture frames above the backrest, where two ancient Scripture verses had been inscribed on parchment:

> *My whole being will exclaim,*
> *"Who is like you, O Lord?*
> *You rescue the poor from those*
> *too strong for them,*
> *the poor and needy from those who*
> *rob them."*
>
> **Psalm 35:10** *(NIV)*

PRACTICAL APPLICATION

For the best results, use a notebook to journal your thoughts and responses as you read the "Practical Application" section near the end of each chapter in Letters from the King.

As you do, listen and write down the insights God speaks into your heart or thoughts through this book, your related prayers, the Bible verses that seem to jump off the page for you, and through people in your life who may wittingly or unwittingly communicate special messages from God to you (2 Timothy 2:7). Pray and search the Bible to verify the authenticity of these messages. After each prayer, take a few minutes and listen for his answers. He does answer; many of us simply have not been taught to pause to receive.

I trust that God greatly enriches your journey with him, as he invites you to walk more fully in your identity as a daughter of the King and as he challenges you to grow confident in your authority as an ambassador for the kingdom.

Have you, like the girl in the story, experienced the feeling of being wrapped-in-a-golden-blanket-of-love from God? If yes, what were the occasions?

If not, where have you seen or felt demonstrations of his great love, protection, and care for you?

What were your thoughts and feelings at each occasion?

How did each experience of God's love impact your faith and actions?

How are those experiences shaping your priorities and actions today?

What parts of your life need to know and feel that love now?

Are you weighted down with stress? Shame? Guilt? Loneliness? Fear? Consider these stunning statistics:

STRESS
- 92% of working women are stressed
- 89% of stay-at-home moms are stressed, overwhelmed by the work they do

What do women report as the physical symptoms of stress?
- extreme fatigue (64%)
- anxiety (59%)
- unhealthy weight gain/loss (44%)
- depression (43%)
- insomnia (36%)
- migraines (19%)

SHAME
Shame is increasingly recognized as a powerful and potentially dangerous emotion. The less we understand about the origin of the shame we experience, and how to deal with it, the more powerfully it manifests in our lives. Overall, shame creates in us a feeling of *being wrong* versus guilt, which is doing something wrong. As we begin to believe the lies that shame whispers in our ears, we become our own worst critics. I call it our self-destruct demons.

> As Brené Brown, a shame and empathy researcher at the University of Houston Graduate College of Social Work, put it: "Shame lurks in all of the familiar places like manhood, family, parenting, money and work, mental and physical health, addiction, sex, aging, and religion."

GUILT
Feeling guilty, is an emotion most women—even highly successful, well-balanced and seemingly I've-got-my-act-together women—experience. The statistics below tell the story: women who have successful careers outside of the home, feel guilty for not spending enough time with their families. On the other hand,

stay-at-home moms feel guilty about not earning money to help with the family expenses. Women all over the world tell me they are very good at finding reasons to feel guilty about something.

- 96% feel guilty at least once per day
- 51% of moms working outside the home feel guilty about not spending enough time with their children
- 55% of stay-at-home moms feel guilty about not making a contribution to the family finances

LONELINESS
Loneliness (feeling distant from other people) has doubled in the past decade—coinciding with the era of online social networking.

FEAR
- 49% of women fear losing all their money and becoming a homeless bag lady

How often do you wrestle with stress, shame, guilt, loneliness, or fear? What steps might you take to open those places to the healing love of your heavenly father?

If you are uncertain what steps to take, know that God wants, more than anything, a close loving father-daughter relationship with you. He wants you to be confidently secure, knowing he created, designed, and accepted you as his daughter. It is his vision of you that ultimately determines and affirms your identity.

You are not an orphan. You do not face the world alone. Quite the opposite. God has adopted you as his daughter, and invites you into his embrace. The first step toward opening yourself to the healing love of your heavenly father is admitting your desperate need for him.

God also blesses you with family, friends, counselors, places of safety, books, and many other resources. Allow these means of God's healing love to help you wipe away the negative "mud" from your past and free you to accept your identity as his cherished, adopted daughter. Accept that God has already accepted you. His arms are open. His embrace is waiting. Yes, for *you*.

Prayer

Dad, I confess that I am in desperate need of knowing you and your love at the core of my being. I bring my stress, shame, guilt, loneliness, and fear before you. I ask that you heal me in every way: emotionally, spiritually, mentally, motivationally, and relationally. Open the eyes and ears of my heart so that I realize I am your cherished daughter. I thank you that you hear—and answer—my cries to you. In Jesus' name. Amen.

THE REQUEST

The king had only one child, I reflected as I walked past welcoming yet vacant rooms, and he longed to adopt many more to share in his great kingdom.

Years ago, he had many adopted children. As they had grown older, they began to doubt his wisdom and despise his laws, the laws he had established to keep them safe and happy.

Despite their rejection, he loved them.

Yet because of their disobedience and lack of trust, the righteous king had considered banishing them from his kingdom. The king's orders would have been quickly carried out, for his power was great. However, the king's only son approached him and begged for mercy on behalf of all the adopted children.

Because of this, the king had compassion on the adopted children and had let them remain on the land he owned. However, they were no longer allowed to enter the castle walls unless they recognized the deep, deep love and fatherly protection of the king and vowed to walk in his wisdom and ways.

As time passed in the land, the king's children had come to ignore his guidelines completely. Finally, they not only rejected the king's ways; they forgot him. Now, much of the king's land was corrupt. But the king's heart would always be for his children.

The day that I met him, he had set out for the sole purpose of finding a child who needed to be adopted as his own. I had been ready when he called my name. My adoption took place many happy years ago. Since then, I have grown up, gotten married, and now have children of my own.

As I continued toward my father's throne room, I was once again overwhelmed with gratitude and love for the one who rescued me and invited me into his home. I entered the brilliant, grand room and greeted my father in the same way I have since I was a child: "Hello, Daddy!"

As always, he received me with a massive, warm hug that only my dad could give. Today, however, his loving eyes smiled differently. There was an unmistakable tenderness about them, and I knew he had something to tell me. Although I could always sense the wisdom behind the words of my father, I seldom could understand his reasons. I knew this would be one of those talks.

"What's the matter, Daddy?"

"My darling daughter, you know how deeply I love you and how much I treasure you, as I do all my children. Very few are even aware that I exist, let alone that I care for them." The king's eyes held a look of both longing and frustration.

"Daddy, I know you exist. I know you care for me. You don't ever have to doubt that I love you."

"I do not doubt you, Daughter. It is just that even though I cherish your love, my desire is for all my children to know of my love for them and for them to live full lives with deep meaning and purpose. I would like you, as my daughter, to go to them, to live among them as an ambassador, and . . ."

I couldn't let him finish. "Go? To them?" I burst into uncontrollable tears with the shock of the news. I had heard that many of those who no longer acknowledged the king were wandering, lacking deep meaning and purpose in life. They lived so very, very far away from here. If my husband, children, and I were to leave, we would no longer live where we could see my dad face to face. No. I did not want anything to change.

He did not reply, and embraced me once again.

MY FATHER'S WORDS

In my heart, I heard him say, *"My children give me joy when they are concerned about my family everywhere. They please me when they are compassionate and willing, when it lies within their power, to alleviate suffering. They please me greatly when my concerns become their concerns, and thus they share in my sufferings. Then my heart rejoices because together we are sharing the work of my Kingdom. Those who do this will one day reign with me.*

"My love for my children is everlasting. It does not waver."

My eyes looked beyond his shoulder to the wall of the throne room, where I saw another elegant, golden picture frame positioned between two tall crystal windows. I read the letters of the Scripture verse inscribed on the parchment.

> *We are therefore Christ's ambassadors, as though God were making his appeal through us.*
>
> **2 Corinthians 5:20a (NIV)**

Practical Application

Journal your responses, and God's inspired insights, to the following:

Webster defines an ambassador this way: (1.) an official envoy; especially a diplomatic agent of the highest rank accredited to a foreign government or sovereign as the resident representative of his or her own government or sovereign or appointed for a special and often temporary diplomatic assignment, (2.) an authorized representative or messenger.

Have you ever thought of yourself as an ambassador for God's kingdom?

If you were to see yourself as God's ambassador, what might your mission be?

How might seeing yourself as an ambassador change the way you approach the following:
    your work?
    your family relationships?
    your marriage?
    your finances?
    your hobbies?
    your entertainment choices?
    your neighborhood?

What changes might you consider making to be a more intentional ambassador?

PRAYER

Dad, I admit I get set in my ways and am comfortable with the status quo. I desire to walk in step with you, wherever you are leading and whenever you are moving. I ask you to give me the courage to trust you, even when the future seems too dark or dangerous. I know you are wise, loving, and gracious, and you always know what is best for my family and me. Here I am. May your way always be done. Amen.

THE SHOCK

Even so . . .

"Go? To *them*?" I repeated. Without waiting for his answer, I asked, "What do you mean? Me? An ambassador? I'm not trained to be an ambassador. I don't know what I would do or what I would say." I rambled on in disbelief, "How can my family and I live outside the castle? We don't have a house, or any means of support. We will be alone in a new and different land." It would be like the days before the king had found me! "Plus what happens if the people hate me?" I ended my tirade with, "We love it here! We need to be by your side! It feels impossible to leave you!"

Patiently, my father addressed my questions. "My son has paved a pathway between the castle and the many villages. The time is right for you to live among my people as an ambassador of my kingdom. When they see you—you, who were once a poor peasant child lacking as they do—expressing my love and compassion for them, it will be as if the king himself is proclaiming his own love to them."

He took my hands in his. "Do you see? I have given you a new life so that you can, in turn, give *them* a chance at a new life with me."

Not persuaded, I exclaimed, "Daddy, I remember from my childhood that many didn't even believe that you are the king! They won't accept your message!" This was such an impossible task! How did my father expect me to make a difference in the lives of people who were so uninterested in him?

"That is very true. It will be difficult for you, my daughter. I guarantee that you will at times be overwhelmed by their evil ways and their lack of understanding. You must always remember that you are my daughter. While you grew up enfolded in my protection and care, you loved to tell others how excited you were that I had adopted you as my own. Now be a living example of my love. Share with others that I want them to know my love and caring. Share with others the Great Story— that my son has paved the pathway between the villages and here so that all may be able to live with me. I want each person to live radiantly as my adopted child."

I could only stare at him in helplessness. I did not know how to be an ambassador. Without him by my side, without the guidance I had come to rely upon, I would feel so alone, so unfamiliar with the strange land I was about to enter.

Knowing my thoughts, my father assured me, "You will not be alone, Princess. I will send my advisor with you, to guide you in all things. He knows my thoughts and my ways. Consult with him in everything, and he will teach you all you need to know. Know that I am the God of the impossible."

MY FATHER'S WORDS

In my heart, I heard him say, *"How beautiful are the feet of those who bring good news in the far and distant places of the world! I will be their constant companion. My presence and guidance will be their stronghold."*

My gaze lowered to the marble tile floor we stood upon. Across the marble a verse was etched in large, sweeping letters so that it could be read when leaving the throne room.

> *How beautiful on the mountains*
> *are the feet of those who bring good news,*
> *who proclaim peace,*
> *who bring good tidings,*
> *who proclaim salvation,*
> *who say to Zion,*
> *"Your God reigns!"*
>
> **Isaiah 52:7 (NIV)**

PRACTICAL APPLICATION

Journal your responses, and God's inspired insights, to the following:

At some point, most of us experience a challenge, whether at work or at home, so great we feel it is almost impossible to handle. When have you experienced such a challenge?

In your journal, list the event. If you have faced more than one, list each of them.

What were your thoughts and feelings as each of these challenges arose?

What about each event made it seem impossible?

At what point in each event did you begin to see God at work?

How do you think or feel God used this challenge to teach or strengthen you?

Are you experiencing one of those "impossible" times now?

In your journal, consider writing a Dear God Letter, including your Impossible List. Are you willing to accept the challenge of trusting God with your list, that he is indeed the God of the Impossible?

PRAYER

Dad, I acknowledge I often let the crisis of current circumstances and the fear of the future overwhelm me. I have tried to solve these issues using my own ways. It's not working. I want to trust you with my Impossible List. I have nowhere else to turn. Help me to be open to your wisdom, insight, and discernment in every situation. Thank you for always responding whenever I cry for help. You are indeed good. Amen.

THE CALLING

Still struggling to fully grasp what my father was asking me to do, I looked at him with fear and anxiety.

Patiently, he repeated, "Daughter, I am sending you into a dangerous place. The people have forgotten about me. They are confused. They have strange ideas about what is right and wrong. They are searching for meaning and purpose in all the wrong places. I am sending you to go and be 'me' among them."

"Father, I don't even fully know your ways yet. How am I to survive without you, in this new place?"

"You know how I sometimes call you 'my precious princess'?" my father asked. I nodded. "Well, that is because I am the king and you are my daughter. I will not leave you to this difficult task alone. As I said before, I am sending my advisor to go with you. He will always be there for you to consult. No matter what the circumstance, he will be with you giving you my advice. He has been with me forever; he knows my ways, and he knows my thoughts. It will be as if I am with you."

I trusted my father's wisdom. However, I did not trust myself. I felt sure that if I stepped away from the castle where I felt safe to become this "ambassador," I would fail in my mission. I had no idea what an ambassador was supposed to do. I was afraid that I would either conform to the ways of those around me, or hide if people laughed at me when I proclaimed my father's love, acceptance, and forgiveness. It would undoubtedly sound ludicrous to people who did not even believe that my father existed. I couldn't possibly tell them that I was actually a princess!

Finally, I said, "I guess you're not asking me. You're telling me, aren't you, Father?" I already knew the answer to my question.

"Daughter, most definitely," he said with a gentle smile.

As his words sank in, another horrifying thought sprang to mind. My husband and children—surely they wouldn't be willing to uproot their lives and come with me on this mission. I couldn't leave them behind either. Oh, what would we do?

As if anticipating my question, he said, "Your family will go with you."

I began to panic. How would I raise my kids without the protection of the castle walls and without the king at their sides? Perhaps they would forget him, too. How would my husband react? He would have to give up his job as the royal financial consultant and start over in a place where no one knew him or his work. He would undoubtedly be hesitant to embark on the mission my father had given not only to me, I now saw, but to my entire family.

Yet I felt urgency in my father's words. In his face, his concern for his people was clear. I grew resolved not to let him down. He had always done so much for me, I thought. This was something I wanted do because of my love for him.

"How long do we have to get ready?" I asked.

"You will never feel ready," my father said wisely. "This mission is not a project to be developed, executed, and accomplished, but a lifestyle to be learned, practiced, and lived. You will leave within the next few days."

Beginning to catch a glimpse of the mission, I hesitantly asked, "Daddy, what do you want me to tell the people when I get there?"

His eyes softened even more, and he longingly sighed. "Tell them that even though they do not know me, I love them. That I care for them, and I am coming to visit them soon."

"Most don't even believe that you are the king," I responded skeptically. "They will not accept the message."

"That is very true, Princess," he said. He went on. "It will be difficult for you because of their unbelief. However, you are my daughter, and no one can change that. I guarantee that, at times, you will feel overwhelmed with their confusion. You must always remember my message and consult with my advisor. You have my calling."

From the pocket of his robe he pulled out a rolled parchment tied with a ribbon the color of garnet and gave it to me. I took the parchment from his hand, removed its ribbon, unrolled the paper, and silently read:

The Calling

I am calling you,
I am anointing you,
I am setting you apart for a divine plan.
Rise up. Walk in it.

Behold,
I make all things new.
Turn your back on old ways.
I open new vistas and new opportunities.
Walk in confidence.
Rest in my calling.

I rolled the precious paper again and slipped it and the ribbon into my pocket. I already knew I would keep it forever, to read the inspiring words again and again.

MY FATHER'S WORDS

Within my heart, I heard him say, *"Child of the wilderness places, know that the desert is also mine. I will bring forth roses out of dry and barren ground when you permit the rivers of living water to flow through you.*

"My children believe in miracles, for they themselves are miracles. Their lives show forth resurrection power. They have seen the work of my hands and believe that I am all powerful. They do not believe in 'impossible.' They trust me to do what no one else can do.

"I am the God of the impossible. It is my joy to do for them what others cannot do. Trust me. In my time, fruit will be born."

My eyes lifted to my father's, and I remembered a Scripture passage he had taught me long ago.

> ***And we know that in all things God works***
> ***for the good of those who love him,***
> ***who have been called according to his purpose.***
>
> **Romans 8:28 (NIV)**

Practical Application

Journal your responses, and God's inspired insights, to the following:

When you read "The Calling," what parts, if any, speak directly to you?

When you read My Father's Words, what parts, if any, speak directly to you?

What action, if any, do you feel God inviting you to take based on "The Calling" or My Father's Words?

What parts of your life need the reassurance of the advisor's peace and direction?

Prayer

Dad, I acknowledge that I often go on my own path and don't rely on your insight and power. I don't want to be that way anymore. I want to walk hand-in-hand with you, on your path. I want to be convinced of the call that you have on my life, and confident that you are opening the doors for the future. Thank you for you are at work deep within me so I am becoming who you say I am, the daughter of the Most High King. May your name be praised in all I do and say. Your daughter. Amen.

THE
FIRST ⟋ LETTER
TO THE KING

JOB HUNTING

Hello, Daddy,

Let me report the good news first. There are many here who know you love them and care for them. They are great people. Yes, they struggle with life's happenings, but they have a sense of contentment about them. They are good, caring, loving people. You will be pleased when you meet them, for they truly are helpful and kind. They have your character.

How do you do that, Dad? How is it that the people who know you are so much like you? They read the letters you sent them many years ago, and strive every day to live according to the wise guidelines you sent. They pour over those letters as if they are gold, seeking to glean every word of insight and encouragement you wrote. They *love* your letters.

Your people have treated us very well. They have helped us to find a home, get settled, and are showing us around this country. Even though they have been wonderfully kind, I must confess that all is not easy. In fact, life here is extremely difficult at times.

There are other people who are *so* confused and have such strange ideas. They don't even want to hear about you. Some laugh in my face. Others just ignore me; they look right through me. No one has tried to physically hurt us yet, for which I am thankful. But they certainly don't believe that you are, or ever were, the king.

Another thing, Father, you sent us here to this land with no source of income to purchase the food, shelter, and clothing we need to live here. So, I'm looking for a job. Frankly, it confuses me, Daddy. I don't understand why you sent us here with nothing!

Well, actually, the more I think about it, it's probably okay. Getting a job to help my husband earn our way in this new country will bring me in contact with more people who need the meaning and purpose that comes from knowing you. I also think that if people were able to see me working and acting as you would work and act if you were here, perhaps it will give them a glimpse of who you truly are. In this way, the message that you love them, care for them, and are coming back soon will be more believable.

So, I'm off to find a job. Do you have any suggestions about what I should do? There are so many choices, Father, that it's almost overwhelming.

Thank you for sending your advisor along with me. He's extremely helpful to talk to. You're right—he thinks exactly like you do, Father.

~ *Your loving daughter*

MY FATHER'S WORDS

After I folded the letter, in my heart I heard him say, *"There are no creatures in my creation that do not struggle to gain the necessities of life. All must do this. It is my plan for creatures great and small. The struggle may differ from the polar bear to the ant and from the* ostrich to the hummingbird, but each works to gain the necessary food and drink.

"My children too must work to gain the necessities of life. It is not good that others provide what you should labor for. If you have more than is necessary, thank me, and give to those who are weak, sick, or unable to work. In so doing, the plan for your existence is accomplished and has purpose.

"Despise neither hard labor nor long hours of toil. By this, you will feel accomplishment, and I will be glorified. Meditate on my goodness. Your faith will increase, and you will be happy and rejoice, child of mine. The world will be attracted by your peace and your joy."

I addressed my letter, and then rose from my place under a shade tree. A few cottages away, the road ended and the path began that led through forests and wilderness to the distant castle. There I saw the man who often tended the path near the village, laboring with a rake to smooth the trail.

I had spoken to him before when I had gone on walks and passed by him. Seeing me, he waved a hand, and I walked over.

"Sir, do you know the way to the castle?" I asked. "I've noticed that you maintain this part of the trail, but I've haven't seen you leave the village."

"Yes, I know the way." He saw the letter in my hand addressed to the king. "I often carry letters between the villages and the castle, and I'll be leaving again soon. Would you like me to deliver yours?"

I thanked him and gave him my letter. A short time later, he left with one sack of provisions and another sack stuffed with letters from town. He followed the trail he had recently raked clean for travelers.

I watched him begin his journey with a purposeful walk. Seeing such dedication, I turned to observe similar efforts of the good people working in their gardens and tending their sheep and cows. I was reminded of a verse from Scripture that had often filled me with inspiration.

> *Therefore I . . . implore you*
> *to walk in a manner worthy of the calling*
> *which you have been called,*
> *with all humility and gentleness,*
> *with patience, showing tolerance*
> *for one another in love,*
> *being diligent to preserve the unity for the Spirit*
> *in the bond of peace.*
>
> **Ephesians 4:1-3 (NASB)**

PRACTICAL APPLICATION

Journal your responses, and God's inspired insights, to the following:

In the Garden of Eden, God gave the work of taking care of the garden to Adam and Eve. They found satisfaction and enjoyment in the results of their labors, their God-assignment. When we work, whether it's paid or unpaid, we are participating in God's plan for us, for our neighbors, and for the world. However, it can also be overwhelming or discouraging to find work that fits us well.

What work do you find most rewarding?

How can you use your gifts and talents to serve others?

What types of situations and activities energize you? What de-energizes you?

When do you feel "in the zone"? Or when have you had a this-is-what-I-was-made-for feeling?

Where have you had positive encouragement from family, friends, or coworkers regarding your work, whether paid or unpaid?

Prayer

Dad, I am thankful for the work that you've given me to do, whether it relates to my family or to my job. I often grumble and am ungrateful for all you provide. I want to change and to be filled with gratitude, to see the incredible opportunities you bring my way every day. I want to embrace each moment as a gift from you. As I work, I trust people will see your character in me. Thank you for continuing to teach and guide me, never giving up on me. You are so good. May your kingdom go forward. Amen.

THE
FIRST LETTER
FROM THE KING

SPREADING THE MESSAGE

My darling daughter,

It was so good to hear from you. Even though I know you have been raised and nurtured with the utmost care and that my advisor is with you, I am still concerned about you and long to see you.

I am *so* glad you found my people and that they are seeking the truth. It must be hard for them also. Daughter, I want you to encourage them. Motivate them, not only to keep living lives that express my love, but also to keep spreading my Great Story—that my son laid down a trail from the villages to the castle, and that I want everyone to come dwell in my presence and to be adopted.

I imagine it would be easy for them to feel frightened by all the turmoil that is happening in the land. They must gather together often to encourage and strengthen each other, so that they can overcome their fears with confidence, and boldly reach out and serve those around them.

Constantly remind them I am coming back soon, and that I both invite and challenge them to tell their own families, neighbors, colleagues, and coworkers about my return. I want to find my land in good condition, not trampled by those who do not know me.

It was a difficult decision on my part, Princess, to send you as an ambassador to an unfriendly land. However, I know you. I have equipped you with the perfect gifts and talents to accomplish my purposes and plans. I know your heart. I know your ways. I know all about you, my daughter, and you can handle this assignment . . . as long as you work closely with my advisor. You are young, but he has been with me from the very beginning and knows everything that you need to know. Wisdom comes from spending time with him and listening to his guidance.

A job. Now that is a tough one, indeed. My guess is that you will enjoy many things since you are so talented. What criteria are you using to choose the right job for you and your family, Daughter?

I look forward to hearing from you again soon. My heart longs to see you.

Be confident. I wrote a poem to help you remember my trust in you.

Confidence

Go in confidence.

I am calling you.
I am choosing you.
I am giving you
my favor,
my power,
my wisdom,
as you walk in my

power,
purpose,
and
presence.

I am drenching you in my anointing,
so that your core being knows my acceptance.

Walk always as my representative.
You are a daughter of the Most High King.

Go in confidence.

~ Your caring father

MY FATHER'S WORDS

I smiled as I read his inspiring letter. In my heart, I heard him say, *"My knowledge of each of my children is perfect. I put each one in the place that is best suited to him. I do not put goats in green pastures and cattle on rocky mountainsides."*

I rose from the bench where I had been reading, lay the letter on the seat, and held it there—safe from any gusts of wind—with a smooth stone I'd found in the garden. Then, my husband, children, and I joined the many families walking to our meeting place. As one, we would read letters the king had sent to his children long ago.

As the families walked, they sang verses of praise from Psalms. We sang with them, loudly, in great joy and confidence.

> *O Lord, you have searched me*
> *and you know me.*
> *You know when I sit and when I rise;*
> *you perceive my thoughts from afar.*
>
> *For you created my inmost being;*
> *you knit me together in my mother's womb.*
> *I praise you because I am fearfully*
> *and wonderfully made;*
> *your works are wonderful,*
> *I know that full well.*
>
> **Psalm 139:1-2, 13-14 (NASB)**

PRACTICAL APPLICATION

Journal your responses, and God's inspired insights, to the following:

What are the gifts and talents that God has given you? (Take your time and list as many as you can think of. Ask friends and family for input. You might be surprised at how many abilities others see in you.)

What steps might you take to use those gifts and talents to serve others while working closely with the Holy Spirit? (Note: I have found that it's easy to attempt to do things on my own, without checking in with the Holy Spirit or pausing to listen for his guidance. Have you experienced this?)

Gifts and talents are turned into strengths when they serve the broader family and community, our neighbor. How are yours serving and helping others?

PRAYER

Dad, thank you for equipping me with the perfect gifts and talents to accomplish your purposes and plans. Often I focus these gifts and talents in a wrong direction. Other times I operate in my own pride, without laying them at your feet so they can become strengths that serve others. I ask for your help to shift my mind-set so I am more aware and intentional about how you want to use me to further your kingdom in every situation. I am so thankful that you invite me to be part of your work in establishing your kingdom here on Earth. Amen.

THE
SECOND LETTER
TO THE KING

SEEKING CAREER CRITERIA

Dearest Father,

Thank you for writing so soon. I have read your letter over and over to my children. We love your words.

You asked me about the criteria I am using to find a job. I had hoped you would tell me. Since you didn't, I'd like to run these ideas by you and see what you think.

Because you sent me to tell the people of this land that you love them and care for them, it definitely seems I should work among them. In this way, when they see me working, they will see you.

At least, it's my wish for your character to flow through me in all I do. I hope that in sharing your kindness, gentleness, patience, and caring, those around me will long for the full life they can have in you. Help me to shine your light in these dark places.

So, criterion number one is that my job is to be working in the midst of those who don't know you.

Secondly, my guess is that as you were raising me, you knew you would be sending me here. So, you schooled me in the things I needed to know and gifted me with those gifts that would be particularly useful in this land. Am I correct, Father?

Criterion number two is that I use the knowledge, teachings, and gifts you have given me.

Thirdly, there are many "jobs" that don't seem to honor you at all; they break your wise guidelines for living or they lead people's hearts further away from you.

This makes criterion number three, my career is to be honorable and pleasing to you.

Father, what other criteria should I use?

~ *Your loving daughter*

MY FATHER'S WORDS

As I drew my name across the bottom of the letter, in my heart I heard him say, *"My children are those who love freely—when it is returned and when it is not. I put within them a fountain which gives forth love and praise. When they walk and labor in the light of my countenance, this fountain overflows and its contents spill out to others. It is rich in life-giving properties. It will be the place where many who are lost begin to desire to have such a fountain themselves."*

Still holding the pen, I looked up to the plaque my husband had engraved and hung above the wooden planks of our front door.

> *"For I know the plans I have for you,"*
> *declares the Lord, "plans to prosper*
> *you and not to harm you,*
> *plans to give you hope and a future."*
>
> **Jeremiah 29:11** *(NASB)*

Practical Application

Journal your responses, and God's inspired insights, to the following:

Do you know the difference between Vocation and Occupation? Though both refer to the work we do, they are different. Occupation, from the Latin *accoupatio,* means "to occupy or fill a position." In the other words, to take up space! On the other hand, vocation, from the Latin *vocare,* means "calling."

Sometimes occupation and vocation are more closely aligned. Sometimes they aren't. When they aren't aligned well, we need to be patient, recognizing and honoring our current season of life. Other times, we surprisingly discover our vocation in the midst of our occupation. It's important to be open to how God is developing and forming our character in all of life situations.

Most of us struggle with what we could do and what we should do. Part of our life journey is balancing the concern with fulfilling our life's passions and taking care of necessities.

What is the interaction between "occupation" and "vocation" for you in this season of life?

How does your work, paid or unpaid, match up with the three criteria?

How can you be more intentional about the three criteria, so you more fully participate in God's creative and redemptive work in the world?

How does God's character shine through you, whether it's in your occupation or vocation; whether it's paid or unpaid; or whether it's with family, friends, coworkers, or colleagues?

What strength of character might God be developing or forming in you during this season?

PRAYER

Dad, I often get frustrated—it feels like I'm only doing the things necessary to live, just occupying space. Help me to see the deeper purpose and meaning behind the work that I do, both paid and unpaid. Open my eyes to see the ripple effect of every smile that's shared, kind word that's spoken, and helping hand that's extended. Thank you for calling me to be your ambassador, and for already beginning to answer my prayer beyond what I could imagine. In Jesus' name. Amen.

FAMILY MATTERS

My clever daughter,

You have got it! The work criteria you have chosen are exactly correct! However, there is one addition. I sent you into that land with a husband and children. How are you handling that responsibility? I have sent you to announce my message, and I have also entrusted some very precious people to your tender, loving care.

Families are important. I do wonder, Daughter, why you have not mentioned more of them in your previous letters. Do not forget them. Nurture them, so they will be as bold and confident as you in proclaiming and living my message.

~ Your loving father

MY FATHER'S WORDS

I placed the letter in my wooden box of keepsakes and resumed dusting our small cottage house, thinking over his words.

As I worked, in my heart I heard him say, *"My youngest children are as precious to me as my oldest children. Age makes no difference. I love the little ones in their helplessness, I love those who have the fervency of youth, and I love those who have the mellowness*

*that comes from maturity. Each is an equally precious child. Teach
this to my youngest ones.*

*"When my children are born, I endow each one with great
capacity for love. Tend my young sheep in protected, verdant fields,
so their love is nurtured with yours, and so they grow healthy and
strong in my ways. When your family's love overflows, each of you
will be equipped to show great love to my lost children, that they may
find me."*

I looked over at the lovely keepsake box again, and recalled
the passages my husband quoted when he gave it to me on our
anniversary. I was reminded that we were one flesh. Our dad
is powerful and will accomplish his purposes and plans in our
marriage, while knitting us together.

**A wife of noble character who can find?
She is worth far more than rubies.
Her husband has full confidence in her
and lacks nothing of value.**

**Her children arise and call her blessed;
her husband also, and he praises her:
"Many women do noble things,
but you surpass them all."**

Proverbs 31:10-11, 28-29 (*NIV*)

Practical Application

Journal your responses, and God's inspired insights, to the following:

Our culture relentlessly inundates us with the Super Woman, I've-got-it-all-together message. The glamour magazines, with airbrushed, Photoshopped supermodels, taunt us from every grocery line, movie, television show, and book: "Life can be better when you're tall and slender, with luscious lashes and voluptuous hair."

Their not-so-subtle message is that you have it all together when you look ravishingly beautiful even though you're raising active children, being a dedicated wife, and earning your keep by holding down a job." Yikes! It seems impossible, doesn't it?

The result? Many of us feel ashamed that we aren't living up to the Super Woman image. Others of us try balance this falsetto image with the competing cry of our true heart.

In the battle, sometimes those closest and dearest to us get hurt or forgotten.

How do you react to the Super Woman I've-got-it-all-together message, honestly? Where in your life are you inadvertently buying into the message?

In what ways do you try to do and be it all? List them.

For each, write whether it fulfills you, or adds to your stress.

How might these activities or practices be keeping you from embracing your true identity as a Daughter of the King?

What activities or practices could you change in order to be more authentically your true self?

What activities or practices could you change in order to be more present with your family?

PRAYER

Dad, I confess. It's easy to fall into the trap of wanting to be who others say I should be. I need your help to more fully recognize my true identity, for I am the most powerful and purposeful when being the real me, not the fake me. Help me also to prioritize those close to me, my family. Respecting my husband and caring for my family are the highest callings I have, even though they are the toughest tasks of all. I want to invest in family relationships so that your love and character is reflected in all we are as a family. I am so grateful that you give me the assurance that you are always there when I cry, "Help." You are a good father. Amen.

THE
THIRD LETTER
TO THE KING

GETTING OFF TRACK

Dear Father,

Thank you for your letter, although I must say it was rather short. I waited so long and anxiously for your letter . . . and then when it arrived, it was just a few paragraphs! However, I won't complain; I love hearing from you.

Thank you for asking about my family. That really is a tough one. My husband is often distracted with trying to provide for us financially. I guess I would be preoccupied as well, in his place, for he has much responsibility.

I worry about him, Father. It's so difficult for him to keep everything balanced between earning money for our shelter, food, and clothing, and being with us. Then, at his job, he has so many demands on him that sometimes he dwells on those issues even when he is at home with us. I deeply miss the closeness we used to share.

It seems his job is so demanding that he doesn't even have time to think about you anymore or the reason we were sent here—to be ambassadors and messengers of the Great Story.

It's difficult for me to admit this, but I also catch myself getting so busy with day-to-day living that I find it difficult to remember the reason we are here. Sometimes just taking care of the kids overwhelms me. They see the ways of this land, in which sensuality, self-indulgence, and violence have become mediums of entertainment and are pressed on them daily by peers, and their memories of you are fading. They are getting caught up in the ways of the world.

Frankly, Dad, I don't think we are doing that well. My husband is terribly busy providing for us, my children don't seem to remember you very well, and I feel alone. I don't know what to do to change the situation and to bring us back to our original mission.

What should I do? I wish so much that you would send for us soon. I miss you more than I can say.

~ *Your loving daughter*

MY FATHER'S WORDS

As an ambassador, wife, and mom, I felt like a failure. My family and I kept getting far off course, and it seemed as if all my efforts were for nothing. At a loss for what else to do, I sat down alone and cried.

Then in my heart, I heard my father say, *"Be still, and know that I am God.*

"My children delight me when they talk with me continually, asking for my wisdom and my way. What a joy it is to have children who desire to please me more than anything else! They shall have the desires of their hearts."

I wiped my eyes, and then opened a collection of ancient Scriptures on my lap. This is the verse that met my gaze.

> ## "But seek first the kingdom of God and his righteousness, and all these things will be added to you."
>
> **Matthew 6:33 (ESV)**

PRACTICAL APPLICATION

Journal your responses, and God's inspired insights, to the following:

Sometimes it's difficult to confess when we feel sad, overwhelmed, angry, hurt, or ashamed. Other times, it's confusing because we feel all of those feelings at the same time! Then, to complicate the problem, it can be challenging to find a secure place or safe people with whom to confess, discuss, and craft a helpful go-forward plan. It may seem easier keeping on the I've-got-it-all-together Super Woman mask.

Here's the most amazing phenomenon I've discovered: when I finally take off my mask, reveal my real self, and cry from the core of my being, "God, help!" he is always faithful to hear my cry and respond. Always.

What spiritual practices or rhythms do you have to help you understand what you're *really* feeling?

If you don't have such spiritual practices or rhythms, here are a few ideas to stimulate your thinking.

- Find a place where you enjoy being and where you feel close to God. For many, that place is in, or in view of, nature—God's creation. Have a conversation with your loving father about your current situation, asking him to help you understand what he wants you to learn about himself, yourself, and the world around you. Remember to read his Word and listen for his insights and direction. He may guide you to discuss with others. Remember to keep working until you have an action plan in response to your new insights. You may even ask someone to be your accountability partner to check your progress in responding to God's fresh words for you.

- Bring your journal along with you when you know you might have some waiting time in the day. Write a Dear-God letter. You might be surprised about how writing can help you to more clearly understand the situation and what you're really feeling and thinking. Listen for his insights and direction. Write the inspirations that come to you as well as the action steps. Read past journal entries to get a broader view of where God is speaking in your life.

- Talk with a trusted Christian friend who is mature in faith and who can help you to discern your thoughts and feelings. Ensure you not only reflect and discuss, but you chart a plan to move forward based on your God-inspired insights. Ask this person to hold you accountable to your plan.

PRAYER

Dad, I often try to hide my frustration and despair with my
I've-got-it-all-together mask. Underneath the mask, I think no
one cares about what I'm really thinking and feeling. That isn't
true, is it? I am so humbled that you want to know what's really
going on with me and where I am really struggling. With your
help, I will change; I will be honest with you, nakedly honest.
I'm so grateful that you listen and you care deeply. I trust you to
care for my heart and help me prioritize life. Help me, O Lord.
Amen.

THE THIRD LETTER

FROM THE KING

STAYING FOCUSED

My daughter,

Thank you for the honest assessment of your situation. It certainly sounds like you may be steering off course, my precious princess. Be careful not to be too busy, for then you will not be walking in the best I have for you. Since I am not there, I trust you are discussing all these issues with my advisor. I know he will be able to see what needs to be corrected.

It is always difficult to balance the many demands of living in a foreign land. It is most important that you do not get too comfortable or drawn in by their worldview.

Talk often with my advisor. I also encourage you to get together with my people regularly, as they have lived in this land longer than you. Many have learned how to live among the foreigners with balance and effectiveness. I know the struggles you endure, since I have endured them myself. My people know them, too. They can help inspire you to meet each day with the joy that comes from dwelling in my land among my followers, and from sharing my love with those who are in need of the meaning and purpose that comes from knowing me.

Read the letters that I send to you, and especially read the letters I sent to my people many years ago. Read them often.

Those letters are filled with my words, insights I shared with my people about how to live in the foreign land without becoming entangled by it.

I caution you, my tender one, do not become confused by the thoughts of that land. Many in leadership do not know me and are seeking to discourage and quiet those who still believe that I love them, care for them, and am coming back soon. Oh, I know there is no way that you will become one of them! However, I know their ways are subtle, and even their clever lies can destroy your success in carrying out my mission.

I sent you to that land for only one reason: to tell them I love them, I care for them, and I am coming to visit soon. Always keep that in mind so your life radiates my character.

Judge all your behaviors, actions, and dreams by that mission. Know that the good that comes from walking in my ways is for you to share with those you meet on every road you travel.

Yes, it is difficult for your husband. He has many pressures; support him in every way possible. The best way to help him stay focused on the mission is for you to stay focused on the mission yourself. Again, I encourage you to talk often with my advisor, even about your husband, as he is experienced in spotting thoughts and ideas that are contrary to the mission. He is very astute in these matters, having been trained in the art of warfare. He has fought and won the greatest battles.

Daughter, I told you in the beginning that this was a dangerous mission. Truly you have entered a war zone. Those in the foreign land will seek to win you over to their way of life and thinking. Remember that you are already a princess, but you are also a queen in training. You *must* stay focused. Keep your eye on the goal always. I love all and want them to hear the message I send to them through you and to experience my care that flows through you.

~ *Your loving father*

MY FATHER'S WORDS

I had paused in my task of milking our cows to read the letter the kind messenger had brought. When I had begun work, all had seemed cloudy and gray. Now the shadows began to lift.

Then in my heart, I heard my father say, *"Child of this present world, the difficulties are great for you. Doubts and discouragements come to you. The entrance of many false doctrines gives rise to much darkness in this world. Look to me, not to the darkness. In the light of my countenance, you will find peace and rest.*

"My child, rest in me, trust me, and do not be afraid.

"When it appears that you are not accomplishing great things, remember that my thoughts of great things are different from yours. My thoughts of great things include obedience in small matters as well as large. Rewards are not given according to greatness of deeds, but according to obedience and love.

"The last will be first—do you not remember, my loved one? Do you have fears that tomorrow will be cloudy and dark? Do you not know that when I am with you, this darkness becomes light? This is my word for you, child. I am with you and will keep you in all places.

"Child of mine, tell others about my kingdom of love. Darkness surrounds you, child of the Light. Shine in all your goodness. Shine in love. Let the world see me again."

I set the letter on a hay bale and looked up to observe my neighbors. Some of them tended their cows and sheep as I did, or fed horses, or scattered seeds for chickens, or reset a fence rail. Others ran wild, causing trouble. A few neighbors sat silently on their porches, doing nothing productive at all, as if they no longer believed that anything could bring relief from suffering or sadness.

For the first time in a long time, I saw not challenges, but opportunities to love and to give hope. I had a mission. I could advance it just by being a better neighbor.

I remembered the verse I had read to my children when they asked me why we were moving here, and I began to feel the warmth of the sun pouring down.

> *"For our struggle is not against flesh and blood, but against the rulers, against the powers, against the world forces of this darkness, against the spiritual forces of wickedness in the heavenly places."*
>
> **Ephesians 6:12 (*NASB*)**

Practical Application

Journal your responses, and God's inspired insights, to the following:

We are reminded of the importance of these spiritual practices and rhythms:

- talking often with the advisor;
- reading the letters that were sent long ago, and
- gathering with God's people.

These are important as we grow in spiritual strength and maturity.

God has crafted each of us uniquely; therefore, it seems reasonable that we each have a distinctive pattern in how we communicate with him and how we strengthen ourselves mentally, emotionally, and spiritually. On a scale of 1 to 10 (with 10 being "this works well for me"), rate yourself to discover which of the following spiritual pathways or practices (adapted from *God is Closer Than You Think* by John Ortberg), work well for you:

Intellectual Pathway (Matt. 22:37)
I connect with God through the *Intellectual Pathway* because I:
- enjoy in-depth teaching about God and the Bible;
- study scripture, using concordances and other resources;
- attend lectures by Biblical scholars when possible.
    Rating: _____

Relationship Pathway (Acts 2:42-47)

I feel God's presence best when I'm in a deep relationship with other Christian believers. Some of the ways in which I follow the *Relationship Pathway* include:

- attending local church services;
- being part of a small group;
- participating in community experiences.
  Rating: _____

Serving Pathway (Matt. 25:45)

I choose the *Serving Pathway* to feel God's presence in my life, because:

- helping others comes naturally to me;
- serving others helps me feel fulfilled;
- attending to the physical needs of others is energizing.
  Rating: _____

Worship Pathway (Ps. 122:1)

I choose the *Worship Pathway* to connect with God, because I enjoy the following:

- praise and worship singing;
- praying and singing with others;
- giving God glory and honor on a regular basis.
  Rating: _____

Activist Pathway (Mic. 6:8)

I'm passionate to be involved through action, therefore I choose the *Activist Pathway.* This path suits my spirituality best because I am:

- energizing with a high level of enthusiasm;
- stimulated by challenges;

- flourishing when I'm involved in causes that lead to transformation and social justice.

    Rating: _____

Contemplation Pathway (Is. 26:3)

I prefer the *Contemplation Pathway*. God is most present to me when I:

- remove distractions and have uninterrupted time alone;
- include images and metaphors to help me pray;
- listen to God in silence and solitude.

    Rating: _____

Creation Pathway (Ps. 19:1)

I follow the *Creation Pathway* because I feel God's presence through nature. I enjoy:

- walking in the mountains or at a lakeside for communion with God;
- church camping and outdoor events;
- gardening;
- riding a motorcycle through the great outdoors.

    Rating: _____

⌘

Which spiritual practices and rhythms do you feel the Holy Spirit inviting you to develop further?

How can you be creative in further developing these spiritual practices while you're balancing your roles and responsibilities in this season of life? Be creative!

PRAYER

Dad, I confess that I sometimes try to fit into the mold of who others think I should be or who I think I should be. Thank you for uniquely crafting and designing me with the utmost care. Help me to honor that uniqueness in myself, in my husband, in my children, and in every person I meet. Help me to be continually open and increasingly sensitive to your voice in my life. I ask for your discernment that I may know your voice versus other voices. May I become more aware of your presence in every moment of life so I may grow in gratefulness to you. Amen.

THE
FOURTH | LETTER
TO THE KING

CONCERNING MY CHILDREN

Dear Father,

Thank you, thank you, and thank you. I am so relieved you understand the difficulties of this assignment!

I am very concerned about my children. I wish I were raising them in your court instead of in this foreign land. I am anxious about how to keep them growing in your ways, and not the ways of this land. It seems impossible, Father!

They have made many friends, which I'm happy about. However, it seems they are bombarded every day with messages from a value system that is often contrary to yours. I am afraid. How do I raise them to choose your path? Plus, you sent our whole family to proclaim this message, but they don't have the training that you provided for me. What do I do? I feel that my kids are at risk.

What are your suggestions, Father?

I need to tell you that I continue to be impressed with your people and how they handle the stresses of this culture. Faithfully, they gather together regularly, both as a larger faith community and as small groups in homes, for mutual instruction and encouragement. They share freely with each other and are so willing to help one another. Often they remind each other that the gifts and passionate interests unique to each of them are actually means by which they can share your loving, caring heart with those they connect with regularly.

In addition, they know the importance of staying focused on your mission. This requires them to study your written letters as well as listen to the subtle promptings of the advisor.

~ Your loving daughter

MY FATHER'S WORDS

Through the open kitchen window, I saw my children jump the picket fence into the yard and land with heavy thuds atop the flowers I'd planted. Their friends followed, doing the same, trampling the blossoms into the dirt. Together they laughed and ran toward the house, pushing each other, verbally tearing each other down with cruel names, instead of building each other up with words of encouragement.

I still wanted to be more intentional in their lives, I realized, to lead them in my father's ways, and to help them each develop a strong inner being that is confident of their true identity.

In my heart, I heard my father say, *"Children of mine are priceless. They are worth more than the world to me. Satan cannot touch they who I have sanctified. He cannot give hope, neither here nor in the world to come. He can give pleasure for a moment, but such pleasure passes quickly, and how empty are the hours that follow. Children of mine have pleasure here, and my promise of joy unspeakable in the world to come.*

"My dear one, you have only to ask, and I will deliver. You have only to request, and I will respond. Continue to lay your requests before me. My goodness will never end."

Yes, I wanted to become a more faithful leader and encourager of my children, so that they, as fellow ambassadors to this land, would choose to become faithful leaders and encouragers themselves, following in the ways of the king. How could I overcome the influence of their friends?

I wanted to feel the same joy over my children's path that John spoke of in the Scriptures.

> *"I pray that out of his glorious riches he may strengthen you with power through his Spirit in your inner being, so that Christ may dwell in your hearts through faith."*
>
> **Ephesians 3:16-17a (NIV)**

PRACTICAL APPLICATION

Journal your responses, and God's inspired insights, to the following:

What challenges do your children deal with each day (or often) at home, in the neighborhood, at school, during extracurricular activities, and in places they or your family frequent?

What unique tests do they deal with spiritually? Emotionally? Mentally? Motivationally? Relationally?

Which people in their lives may be challenging to your children's faith? Be honest—include relatives, family friends, your children's friends (and their siblings and parents), teachers, coaches, and others.

What interests, pastimes, or hobbies may be snares to your children's faith? Consider their choices of entertainment, music, games, Internet activities, and others.

In addition, list any habits and behaviors your children have adopted that may be leading them off the path of the king.

As parents, we have the incredible opportunity to become actively involved with our children's faith journey. Especially when they are young, we are mentoring and modeling a faith walk for our children. Therefore, in your journal, freely log all of your concerns. (At the end of the next chapter, we'll explore specific solutions.)

Prayer

Dad, it is easy for both my family and I to get entangled in activities and situations without even thinking about how they fit into your best plans for us. Thank you for the nudge to notice situations where we might be wandering off your path. As I list the challenges in my journal, help me see clearly who, what, and where they are. Thank you for reminding me that your power has no limit, and that your love, for my family and especially for precious children, endures forever. Amen.

THE
FOURTH LETTER
FROM THE KING

PARENTING PRESSURE

Daughter,

Yes, it is difficult to know how to raise children in a foreign land. There is great pressure to conform to the popular ways of thinking. I understand the desire for your children to "fit in" and to be accepted by their friends.

My daughter, you have the privilege of teaching them my ways, just as I have taught you. Raise them to know my ways, to be grateful to show those around them how much I care, and to tell others of my love for them. Right now, I want you to understand the importance of this task. They are precious to me, and I want them to know the strength that comes from knowing me. I understand this is difficult and often seems overwhelming; it is an important responsibility.

In fact, this is one way others will know your story is true: by watching you faithfully, tenderly, and wisely teach and raise your children.

You talked about looking for a job. I submit to you that your job as a mother matches up nicely against the number one criterion you outlined: "My job needs to be out working in the midst of those who don't know you." Absolutely! As you teach and nurture your children, you will be working among those who need my love in order to be fully alive. In your loving, you show your children, as well as those who are watching you, the vibrant life that comes from following my way.

Your children and your friends can see how the clarity of living in the light is so very different from the darkness. In fact, as you train and nurture your children, you will invariably find others who want training and nurturing. You will meet criterion number two that you set for yourself: "I need to use the knowledge, teachings, and gifts you have given me."

You will be amazed, Daughter, at all the opportunities coming your way when you hold training and nurturing your children in the highest regard. Truly, there is nothing more pleasing than training the little ones to come to me. Look at all the time I spent with you, my precious princess. You know from personal experience that my heart is for children.

A child who is properly guided and built up will do much in furthering my kingdom. This meets criterion number three that you set: "The work needs to be honorable work that is pleasing to you."

Daughter, how often do you visit with my advisor about how to raise your children in a foreign land? I encourage you to talk with him often, for he is filled with insight. He has raised many children with brilliant success. He can help you.

I also encourage you again to visit often with my people. They too have much wisdom and will be able to help you sort out what is right for your children.

I am confident you will do the right thing, my darling daughter, knowing that your children are of the utmost importance to me. I would give my life for them. I love them more than you can imagine.

~ Your loving father

MY FATHER'S WORDS

Pressing the letter to my cheek, I quietly pushed open my children's bedroom door, and for a moment watched them as they slept. At the utter peacefulness and sweetness in their faces, my great love and hope for them beat anew within me. No matter what their imaginations intended, I knew that my father would bring about good.

At that thought, in my heart, I heard my father say, *"The story of love is best told by your life. The song of songs is best sung by your manner of living. The tremendous truth of my provision for salvation is best demonstrated by your brokenness over Calvary.*

"Children of mine are exceedingly precious to me. I cannot bear to see any of them suffer unnecessarily. I will heal them in body and spirit. They can trust me to make them well and whole in all ways.

"Again, my children, give me much praise. There is no way to please me more than to exhibit a heart full of genuine praise. This shows a heart that trusts in me. And this is my greatest need—to have you trust me. Praise and trust go hand in hand. Both things are precious in my sight."

Gently, I closed the bedroom door. The children weren't only mine and my husband's, I remembered. They were also children of the king, my father. I wanted my father's continuous guidance so that I would parent them wisely.

Train a child in the way he should go, and when he is old he will not turn from it.

Proverbs 22:6 (NASB)

Practical Application

Journal your responses, and God's inspired insights, to the following:

In the previous chapter, you listed challenges, tests, and snares your children face each day (or often), including relatives, friends, authority figures, entertainment choices, and other activities that distract your children away from God. What are some things that you might do to strengthen your children emotionally, mentally, relationally, and spiritually?

Keep in mind that the coming days, weeks, or months will be a labor of great love and boundless patience, the degree of love and patience God shows when guiding us. Your investment of time and energy will have great reward eternally.

Prayer

Dad, thank you for the awesome privilege of nurturing and training your children. I often get frustrated, even overwhelmed. Thank you for your patience, kindness, and graciousness when teaching me. May I show the same to my children. Help me to model for them a daily walking in your power, purposes, and plans that we might intimately know your peace, joy, and strength. As I move forward on this overwhelming and arduous parental mission, I am assured that your Holy Spirit is always by my side. I cannot do this without you. Amen.

THE
FIFTH LETTER
TO THE KING

MOTHER OR MISSIONARY?

Dear Father,

I am sorry this last letter has been so long in coming, but I have thought long and hard about what you said.

First, I confess I do not talk with your advisor as frequently as I should about this monumental task of raising these little ones. Thank you for reminding me to talk with him. Sometimes I get so busy with doing everyday things that I forget to chat with him about the day's activities, about the best long-term decisions for my family, and about the proclaiming of your message. I know he longs for me to tell him my needs so I don't bear the load myself.

Father, will you ask me that question often? I think I get distracted so easily that I want a regular reminder.

There is something in your last letter that confuses me. We agreed that one of the important criteria in looking for a job is being able to use the knowledge and skills I have. Are you *certain* that if my first priority is raising children, job opportunities (where I can be your ambassador) will come my way?

I don't know, Father. In your messages to me you write that my mission is to practically, tangibly love people and to tell them you care for them, you love them, and you are coming back soon. You write that I, in order to accomplish that goal, need to be out working with people, befriending them and lending a hand. In this way, they will see your character and get to know you, so a relationship can be built with them and they will be receptive to your message. At the same time, you speak of the utmost importance of training and nurturing my children. Can the two truly be done simultaneously? Frankly, it seems impossible.

This is too confusing! How can both projects be of immense importance? A job, or even being neighborly on a consistent basis, requires that I be out in the world. Training my children requires I be at home, tied to them and their activities. I don't get it.

In truth, I recently became so overwhelmed by it all that I became despondent and could hardly get out of bed for days. I feel like such a failure!

I know you're going to ask me if I spoke with your advisor about this. I have cried my heart out to him! He seems to understand . . . but he offers no advice! He can be so frustrating to deal with at times. I want help; he seems to just stand by watching me trip, fall, and get frustrated. I trust you that he is right for this job, Father, but sometimes I wonder about him.

I'm sure you sense that I am frustrated. I don't think I'm doing anything right. I think you sent the wrong daughter for this task. I want to come home! I miss you.

~ *Daughter*

My Father's Words

In frustration, I began to crumple the letter with my hands.

Then, in my heart, I heard my father say, *"My children are those who constantly delight me by their trusting obedience. They care not that others walk differently. They are pleased only when they know they are in my place for them. This place may be the same place they were in last year, or twenty years ago. It is a place of joy for them because they know they are abiding in me, and I am leading them moment by moment. My perfect plan might not identically match the plan you envision, but it is good because it is my plan".*

I sat quietly a bit longer. Once again, I heard words of encouragement in my heart, *"Train my little ones to walk in my ways; they are as precious to me as you, my dearest daughter, and are in need of continuous love and gentle guidance. My little ones are my future ambassadors; they will learn and grow in their calling as they see my love for others displayed in you. You need not choose between 'mother' and 'missionary.' Nurture the little ones, and watch for opportunities to minister to my sheep, who are searching for meaning and purpose. I will send them across your path to receive my comfort through your listening ear, my inspiration through your spoken words, and my healing strength through your welcoming heart."*

I smoothed out the paper, knowing now that my efforts would be empowered.

> *Happy are those who reject the*
> *advice of evil people,*
> *who do not follow the example of sinners*
> *or join those who have no use for God.*
> *Instead, they find joy*
> *in obeying the Law of the Lord,*
> *and*
> *they study it day and night.*
>
> *They are like trees that grow beside a stream,*
> *that bear fruit at the right time,*
> *and whose leaves do not dry up.*
> *They succeed in everything they do.*
>
> **Psalm 1:1-3 (GNV)**

PRACTICAL APPLICATION

Journal your responses, and God's inspired insights, to the following:

With what current situations in your life do you feel frustrated or overwhelmed? Sometimes there are so many that it works to make a list or to sketch a mind map, drawing a bubble or circle for each situation.

What is frustrating or overwhelming about each situation?

What is the core belief or thought that's fueling the negative emotions?

How might you change that belief or thought to be more productive for you, reducing the frustration or giving you a greater sense of control?

What aspects of these situations might you be grateful?

Where are the opportunities each gives you?

Where are you possibly being strengthened?

What blessing is tucked inside each situation?

Next, when you're frustrated, despondent, feeling helpless and hopeless, it can help to make a list of every blessing that comes to mind. During times of depression, it may take all of your creative juices to come up with even one blessing to give thanks. Stretch yourself. If one is easy, go for ten blessings. If ten is easy, then go for a list of 100. Having a grateful heart opens the doors of possibilities and brings love, life, and light into our lives.

PRAYER

Dad, forgive me for the times I complain more than I thank you, for when I overlook good to dwell on only the bad, and for neglecting opportunities to bring others to your healing, waiting arms. In the same way you gathered me up in your embrace when I was still covered in the mud of my poor choices, please, *please* remind me that you still embrace me. It is in knowing your embrace deep in my core that I am strengthened. I heartily praise you for showing me I am both mother and missionary, working to expand the message of your kingdom. Amen.

THE
FIFTH LETTER
FROM THE KING

DELICATELY DESIGNED

Precious Princess,

Oh, my dear daughter, I cried with you when I read your letter. I know your tender heart. I know your intense desire to do what is right and to walk in my way. You desire to be a loving person who shares the life and light of my kingdom. You are so dear to my heart. If you could only comprehend deep in your core how much I love you and care for you. It is because you are so dear to me that I personally trained you.

Honey, I have spent hours and days with you teaching you my ways. They did not come naturally to you. Many times you fought me. You have a very strong independent streak in you; it took tender, loving care and patience on my part to train you. However, know I have prepared you specifically for this mission to love people and to tell the Great Story.

This is one of the most important privileges in my kingdom. I sent you because I see you as someone willing to follow me in spite of opposition and scoffing from a culture rooted in their own, self-absorbed mission. Someone who would believe in me when everyone around them would walk away from me. Someone who would seek to know my heart above all else.

That person is you, my daughter. Yes, it's you. You have a heart of faith and obedience; a heart that knows me and wants to please me with your whole life. You are designed for this purpose. You are designed for my purpose. You must trust me in this, for I have invested much into preparing you. You, with the help of my trusted advisor, can effectively live a life that tells the Great Story. Remember, even when you share a cup of water with the least of these, you share with me.

Thank you for being honest with me. I have found it is easy for many to get distracted. I promise you that I will often ask you about your relationship with my advisor. I also suggest that you talk to my people and find someone who will ask you that same question. It is good to find someone who can hold you accountable on a regular basis. Perhaps that same person can keep you accountable to your mission. You have mentioned it is easy to lose focus.

You also mentioned you have cried your heart out to my advisor and he seems to be unresponsive. May I ask a tough question? Did you take sufficient time to listen for his advice after you finished crying? As I recall, my daughter, you love to talk. If you want his direction, you will also need to be quiet for a while and listen to him.

I understand your frustration with the multiple priorities you have. Sometimes we want everything, including wisdom, *now*, do we not? But, does everything have to come about right *now*? There are seasons in life where the scale must tip in favor of one priority or another, one lesson to learn or another. That does not mean that you leave one part of you locked up or sitting on a shelf. Your main focus is tipped in one direction, but the other priorities provide key motivators for you also. It is a difficult truth to figure out without having times of quiet reflection and abiding with me.

I assure you, Daughter, that when your role as nurturer of your children is in proper perspective, numerous other opportunities will be present. You will be happy beyond measure and will know you are walking the right pathway. As you care for your family, you will find many opportunities to share my story with my wandering children, and tell them that I love them and I am coming back soon.

As I have shown you, working alongside people may mean formally, like at a job, or it may be more informally, as you get to know people in your neighborhood and school. In both places, you can be light.

This has been a long letter, but I sensed your frustration and wanted to respond to it. Remember: Be still and listen.

~ *Your father*

MY FATHER'S WORDS

I sat still and listened. With the advisor's guidance, I could confidently be an ambassador to those who were searching for the meaning and purpose that their king provided and also successfully lead my children. I also realized the importance of embracing this season of life, with its unique challenges and blessings.

A moment later, in my heart, I heard my father say, *"Your life in me is a growing experience. Do not be discouraged when you make mistakes. It is your heart attitude that matters to me. I expect that my children will have to learn many things by experimentation. All children learn step by step. You will avoid many mistakes by listening carefully to me.*

"However, some things are learned only through experience. Through failure you are kept humble and useful. Let failure be just another vehicle in perfecting my image within you. Meditate on my goodness. Your faith will increase, and you will be happy, rejoicing child of mine. Then the world will be attracted by your peace and your joy."

"Be still," he wrote. By "still," I began to understand, he meant my body, my emotions, and my thoughts. If one of the three was restless, then my ability to listen would be impaired. I also began to see that when I became still, the advisor could become active. During these moments of stillness when I accomplished nothing, he could accomplish much.

My father delicately designed me for his purpose. In my still, quiet moments, his advisor will reveal my father's purposes and plans.

> *. . . Let the wise listen and add to their learning, and let the discerning get guidance. . . .*
>
> **Proverbs 1:5 (NIV)**

Practical Application

Journal your responses, and God's inspired insights, to the following:

Rate yourself on a scale of 0 to 10 (with 10 being the highest) on the progress you're making in developing these spiritual practices and rhythms:

_____ Becoming a better listener, waiting for his still, quiet voice?

_____ Growing as a daughter who seeks to know God above all else?

_____ Taking your I've-got-it-all-together mask off when praying?

_____ Crafting an action plan to move forward after discussing your concerns with God?

_____ Spending time in his Word, reading and studying?

_____ Discovering and nurturing your spiritual pathways?

Prayer

Dad, I confess I treat prayer like a fast-food drive-through solution—call out a request, pause at the pickup window for a quick exchange, and then zoom on with my life. Thank you for graciously reminding me that you want more than a drive-through solution: make my requests, turn off the engine, and wait patiently for you. You want to talk often. Thank you, thank you, thank you for your response. Thank you for revealing to me how to listen for your voice. You are so good. Amen.

THE
SIXTH / LETTER
TO THE KING

MESSY MONEY MATTERS

Dear Father,

What would I do without you? You are wonderful! So wise. So loving. You know me so much more than I know myself. It's like you understand my very thoughts, frustrations, and desires. What a wonderful father you are!

You're right. I was crying my heart out to the advisor . . . without taking sufficient time to listen. I'm practicing listening. You know that's a difficult one for me, don't you, Father?

I still want to talk more with him, in depth, about some other issues that are troubling me. I have found he thinks just like you. When I talk to him, it makes me feel like I'm actually at home sitting in front of the fireplace talking with you. Thank you for sending him along with my family and me to this foreign land. Without him, we would definitely be lost.

As you suggested, I did find one of your people who is willing to ask me whenever we see each other about my listening skills and if I am staying focused on the mission. She is a wonderful woman. She loves you. It's the strangest thing, Father. When I talk with her, I almost feel like I'm talking with you, or your advisor. She is so full of love and wisdom. Have you ever met her?

You will be pleased to know that she also has raised children in this foreign land, and that all those children believe in you and love your ways. I think she will be a good resource as I learn how to raise my children in this culture that doesn't appreciate you, their king. Yes, I know, I will also talk with your advisor about raising children—he has clearly been successful on this before!

Father, I have another confession to make. I am very embarrassed, but I'm at the point of major frustration and need your advice. When we first arrived here, we were unsure what to do about housing and all the other items that appeared to be required for living in this land. It is the custom of this land to borrow money to buy these types of things. I imagine that would have been okay, except we have encountered some difficulties.

First, I think we wanted too many things. Everyone else has a nice place to live and nice things inside. It seemed like that was the right thing to do at the time. In hindsight, it would be fair to say that we are justly reaping what we unwisely sowed, since we purchased what we wanted before we could afford it. Also, rather than make choices that you would be pleased with, we focused more on pleasing ourselves.

Then, because of the settling in and the children's needs, I haven't gotten an "outside" job to generate money to repay the loans. My husband has had difficulty in that he does not have the job he is best suited for. Disappointingly, the type of work he has the most talent for doesn't pay enough money to cover our expenses.

Now, as we slowly pay back what we owe, we don't always have enough finances.

I am embarrassed to admit this, Father, but the added stress means I have shouted at my husband a couple of times recently, and haven't been as loving, kind, or nurturing as I want to be. I feel trapped. I think this is why the children/job dilemma has been so intense lately. I feel like I need money, and yet I know that my children are a top priority *and* that I want to be sharing your love and your message with others.

This is the worst bind I've ever been in. I feel like I've made a mistake that will keep me in a permanent snare. If I remain in this tangle, will I ever be able to focus on sharing your message with all my heart, soul, mind, and strength?

~ *Trapped forever,*
Your daughter

MY FATHER'S WORDS

Usually I felt better after writing a letter to my father. I didn't this time. I had faced barriers before, but now I felt trapped in every way.

As before, I waited for his whispered words of guidance to come. I sat still and listened. For the longest time I could hear nothing but my own jumbled thoughts and troubles. Then I remembered that father could always turn bad situations into good, even when my own mistakes had caused the trouble. Knowing this, I grew calmer.

Then in my heart, I heard my father say, *"My perfect knowledge keeps me from error. Trust me to guide and provide perfectly for you. Children of the day, again I say to you, be at peace. The sign of walking in my presence will be that peace rules in your life. No one can deny my presence in a life that exhibits peace.*

"In a valley of shadows, the sun is still shining! You might not see it, you might not even feel its warmth, but it is still there. When the shadows surround you, rest in the assurance that my love is from everlasting to everlasting."

We now had a lot of things like our neighbors had, I reflected. However, we were too stressed about the resulting money mess to be able to fully enjoy the new possessions.

> **"No one can serve two masters.
> Either he will hate the one and love the other,
> or he will be devoted to the one
> and despise the other.
> You cannot serve both God and Money."**
>
> **Matthew 6:24 *(NIV)***

PRACTICAL APPLICATION

Journal your responses, and God's inspired insights, to the following:

In our current culture, the keep-up-with-the-Joneses mentality is alive and well. Many people feel compelled to own things as nice as their neighbors, and to have them *now* (instant gratification). Instant debit and credit cards make it easy for us, even inviting, to step into the steel jaws of that trap. Sadly, this recipe for disaster often leads to credit issues and ongoing stress, sometimes for years. As a culture lulled by the brief, intoxicating high of immediate pleasure, we purchase with our emotions, and then justify the purchase with logic.

Being an ambassador is a whole-life endeavor, even with our finances.

In what ways are you feeling financially trapped?

List unnecessary items that you are frequently tempted to buy (and often do).

Stress, both short term and long term, is significantly reduced when we steer clear of the intoxicating highs of immediate pleasure. What might be some practices you could implement to reduce unnecessary spending and be wiser with your purchases?

PRAYER

Dad, I confess to my addiction to the brief, emotional highs of buying new things. It is like eating "comfort" food that is unhealthy and that leads invariably to additional kinds of stress. I ask you, Father, to train me to be wise in money matters. I want to put the money mess behind me and to move forward with your wisdom, insight and discernment. Thank you for understanding, and for already beginning to help. May all that I do bring happiness to you. Amen.

THE
SIXTH LETTER
FROM THE KING

GLITTERING FALSE GOLD

Daughter,

I am deeply saddened by your letter, my love. As we have discussed, this is a dangerous assignment. The status symbols in each culture have a strange allure, deceiving many into thinking that certain items are "must haves." It surely is a lie. As you have discovered by now, this is one of the quickest and easiest ways to get distracted from your mission.

My guess is that you did not talk with my advisor about your financial decisions. He knows my thoughts concerning this snare. For those who listen to him, he provides great wisdom on how to handle finances. I encourage you, in the future, to discuss all transactions with him. He will provide a balanced perspective that will allow you to meet your needs without becoming trapped in the system of the culture. He will teach you about how to use your money to proclaim the message that I love, I care, and I am coming back soon. Know, Daughter, that people will watch how you spend your money. I must urge you again, to be very careful in this area.

So, what to do now that you are "trapped?" Know that when you err such as this, there are always consequences to be reaped. I am sad to say, you are going to reap difficulty for some time.

First, acknowledge the things you did incorrectly; you relied on your own way, without consulting my advisor. You let the culture and various temptations influence your thinking, instead of remembering the truths I taught you.

Next, decide with firm resolve that in the future, both you and your husband will consult my advisor on all financial matters. Consult *and* take the necessary time to listen! Do not move forward until you have listened and heard.

Then, remember you are only temporary guests in this land. My daughter, you have all the riches in the heavens at your disposal. I know you will agree that nothing in that land even compares in beauty, lavishness, and wonder to the smallest servant house in my kingdom. All this is waiting for you upon your return as a queen. Why waste your time and energy on having the "best" over there? It pales in comparison to the riches I have for you! *Please*, do not get trapped again! Always keep your mission in mind. If you remember to do this, you will be less enticed by the world around you.

All the money must be repaid, my daughter. I encourage you to do so as quickly as possible while remembering to keep your family relationships loving and nurturing. Do all you can to get your finances under control, so you can fully focus again on your mission.

Remember what you have learned, my daughter. I have trained you well. Do not stray from my teachings.

~ *Father*

My Father's Words

I reread his letter, longing for peace and an end to the money mess. After many long moments of waiting, in my heart I heard my father say, *"My thoughts include obedience in small things as well as great. Rewards are not given according to greatness of deeds or possessions, but according to obedience and love. The last will be first—do you not remember, my loved ones?*

"Peace, my children. Peace! Has darkness overwhelmed you, dear ones? Come again to the Light. Do not continue to be occupied with the things of this world and the attractions which are momentary. Give your attention to the things which are eternal. Those will not slip out of your hands or disappear. They become more and more certain day by day.

"The dearest friends of mine are those whose hearts are set to do my will. Their actions may not be perfect, but it is the set of their desires and wills that is dear to my heart."

At least my husband and I are learning to consult with the king's advisor, and to make every effort to avoid getting ourselves into this situation again. We also were learning that the king would not judge us for mistakes, but would lovingly use them to guide us.

Things had brought us stress. Through my father we had peace. The king would always make sure our needs were met, and would always bring beautiful light from dark shadows.

> *"Do not store up for yourselves*
> *treasures on earth,*
> *where moth and rust destroy,*
> *and where thieves break in and steal.*
> *But store up for yourselves treasures in heaven,*
> *where moth and rust do not destroy,*
> *and where thieves do not break in and steal.*
> *For where your treasure is,*
> *there your heart will be also."*
>
> **Matthew 6:19-20** *(NIV)*

PRACTICAL APPLICATION

Journal your responses, and God's inspired insights, to the following:

How will you develop the habit of consulting with the Holy Spirit prior to each prospective purchase, no matter how small the item might be? What spiritual habits and rhythms might be helpful? List several good ideas. Then talk with your family and decide together how best to consult and listen to the king's advisor in all money matters.

God, and only God, will give you the knowledge and strength to make good financial decisions for both the short and long term.

PRAYER

Dad, I desperately need you in the financial area. I want to be a wise steward of all that you've given me. Thank you for showing me the way to overcome my spending addiction—by consulting your Holy Spirit so that my future choices are beneficial to my family and me long term. I give you my desire for new items, and exchange it for your peace that comes from investing in those things that don't turn to dust. I long to live in contented peace and to enjoy a close relationship with you in all things. Amen.

THE
SEVENTH / LETTER
TO THE KING

DOUBLE STANDARDS

Dear Father,

Sorry to disappoint you. As I read your letter, and as I talked
with your advisor (and listened!), I remember your teaching
where you said, "Do *not* conform to the standards and
thoughts of other lands." Then you went on to say I was to be
transformed into your likeness by always renewing my mind.
That's really where it starts, doesn't it, Father? It all starts in my
mind and in my thoughts.

How do I stay pure in this land? Messages that are in direct
contradiction to your teachings shout from every street corner.
"Do what feels good!" "Why deny yourself?" "What is done
in secret remains a secret!" "This is so exciting, it should be
illegal!" No matter where I look or go, there is something or
someone contrary to you. It is so insidious that it even comes
into our house through all the entertainment options offered.
How do I stay pure and yet be engaged with culture enough to
have the credibility to share your message loudly and clearly?

These double standards are very confusing, Father. When
I try to step back and take a look at our situation from your
perspective, I'm not sure we're doing very well in this. I wonder
how we get back to the way you want us to live and be. Help me
to know, deep in my soul, that you are most greatly honored,

people are most greatly served, and I am most greatly fulfilled, when I am serving you in all that I think, all that I do, and all that I am.

I have met a few neighbors and have been able to assist them in small ways, helping one to find a lost pet, loaning another a few eggs for baking. They have warmed to me as a result, and we talk on occasion, but will my efforts lead to any real results? I hope they will, and the advisor assures me that every interaction makes a difference.

Keep me single-mindedly focused on your purposes, your presence, and your plans. Help me to triumph over the double standards that work against me. Most importantly, help me to love so that others will know the refreshing life that you give. Help me to lift high the light of your message.

I always appreciate your thoughts, Father.

~ *Love,*
Your daughter

MY FATHER'S WORDS

Since it was early in the morning and my family had already left the house to go about their day, I went out for a walk in the countryside to refresh myself.

While walking, in my heart I heard my father say, *"My children give me great joy when they withhold nothing from me, and when nothing is more important than following my ways. I will give priceless blessings to those who walk with me in this manner.*

"Have you desired something in prayer? Have you asked and not received? Think not that your desire is unknown to me or that your

wish to avoid a temptation is not known to me. Think rather that my knowledge permits me to choose the best time for the answer. It is not always best for you to receive a prompt answer. Trust me to send the right answer at the right time. What may seem like a long delay to you may be just momentary to me.

"When my children are instant in prayer, I am instant in attention. It is not always best for them that I answer instantly, but they have my attention and my guidance instantly."

I felt refreshed, and I was glad that I had invited the advisor to walk with me.

Therefore, I urge you, brothers,
in view of God's mercy,
to offer your bodies as living sacrifices,
holy and pleasing to God—
this is your spiritual act of worship.
Do not conform any longer to
the pattern of this world,
but be transformed by the
renewing of your mind.
Then you will be able to test and approve
what God's will is—
his good, pleasing, and perfect will.

Romans 12:1-2 (NIV)

Practical Application

Journal your responses, and God's inspired insights, to the following:

What might be some of the ways you are conforming to the beliefs and values of this world?

What might be some of the negative consequences of your resulting behavior?

What steps could you take to be more diligent about renewing your mind so that your thoughts are more aligned with God's gracious ways?

How might you leverage your spiritual pathways to help in this endeavor?

How might your spiritual practices and rhythms help you with this priority?

Consider participating in a weekly group of enthusiastic, dedicated Christ followers who share your interest in seeking God.

Prayer

Dad, it helps so much to know that you are aware of the difficulties I face in being your ambassador. I confess I often fall into the trap of following those who don't honor and respect you. I long to be more like you, to see people and situations from your perspective, to hear the cries of people's hearts, and to do those things that bring honor and glory to you. Thank you for equipping me with the abilities and insights needed to do your work, so that I may be your ambassador with confidence. Amen.

THE
SEVENTH LETTER
FROM THE KING

WALKING IN MY WAYS

Dear Princess,

Your last letter sounds like you continue to be overwhelmed with all the choices and problems before you. It is understandable. You must be confident that there is always an answer. There is always a way for everything to work together to bring out the best in you, your family, and your situation.

There is a requirement on your part, if you want to ensure that goodness is brought out of that which is meant to destroy you. You ask what the requirement is? That requirement is simply this: *Walk in my ways.*

Daughter, I can only provide protection when you walk in my ways. I can only wring success out of perceived failures when you trust me with your whole heart. I can only ensure victory when you are gathering with my people, reading and studying my letters, and spending time with my advisor. Then, and only then, will you be successful in your mission to show those who have wandered away from my ways that I love them and care for them.

Consider this:

Will you let me?

Only I can fill your deep longing.
Money will not.

Recognition will not.
Status will not.
Your husband will not.
Your children will not.
Knowledge will not.
Friends will not.
Success will not.

Only I can fill your deepest longings.
Will you let me?

In your last letter you said, "I wonder how we get back to the way you want us to live and be." You have uncovered a powerful nugget of truth. I am most concerned about your "being"— about who you are on the inside. When your "being" is in line with my principles, then you will walk in joy. When you can "be" me to your friends, neighbors, and coworkers, then they will see my character and be more open and receptive to hearing my words that I have sent to them.

To be most effective in your mission, Daughter, you must ensure that your heart is clean and pure before me. I am extremely confident you will learn and implement these truths. I have always found you to have a heart soft toward me and eager for the truth. I have also sent a letter to my advisor, asking him to be extra diligent to work with you in these areas.

I look forward to hearing what you are discovering. I delight in your letters, and I am pleased that you value talking to me, listening to my advice, and learning my ways.

I love you and I care for you, my darling daughter.

~ Your father

My Father's Words

He is always here for me, I reflected. Always teaching, guiding, listening, and loving. Always. Even when I fail.

Then in my heart, I heard my father say, *"Beloved, diligently watch over your heart. You hear correctly. Root out all of those things that are not of me. I have much work for you to do. It is good for you to start with a freshly cleansed heart. Purity of heart is important to me. You are my chosen ambassador. You will accomplish much in the furthering of my kingdom. Therefore, circumcise your heart. Make it ready to serve me wholeheartedly. I will bless you and use you far beyond your wildest imaginations. You are mine. You are loved.*

"My beloved ones may rest in peace when everyone else is troubled. I give peace that originates in the heart; therefore, it is protected from outward disturbances. My children may have an abundance of peace in every situation. Trust me completely. In this you will find peace."

I paused from turning dirt in the garden to wave to the man who tended the path to the castle and sometimes carried letters between the castle and the villages. He returned the greeting, and then continued selecting small rocks from a pile to line the sides of the path.

If I wanted to find genuine peace, I saw, it would come not from avoiding action, and thereby a possibility of failure, but from trusting in the endless wisdom of my father as I prepared to stride ahead.

And when my "being" came in line with my father's principles, then I would be able to walk in joy. Then my feet would be ready.

My father was creating in me his will. He would likewise show me the way to do it.

> *The Lord will guide you always;*
> *he will satisfy your needs in a*
> *sun-scorched land*
> *and will strengthen your frame.*
> *You will be like a well-watered garden,*
> *like a spring whose waters never fail.*
>
> **Isaiah 58:11 (NIV)**

PRACTICAL APPLICATION

Journal your responses, and God's inspired insights, to the following:

The king says, "I can only wring success out of perceived failures when you trust me with your whole heart." What mistakes or failures in your life might you bring before God so you could be healed, set free from the pain, and transformed with new vitality and energy?

How can you use past failures, and the wisdoms gleaned from them, to more closely walk in God's ways now?

When life seems chaotic and messy, and when you feel like a failure, that's the time to press into your relationship with God. What might you do to be more open and transparent with God?

PRAYER

Dad, my life seems to be riddled with ways that I've failed myself, disappointed others, and offended you. I bring all those mistakes to you so that you can pull forth the golden nuggets. These tested-with-fire-in-the-crucible-of-life lessons enrich not only my life but also the lives of my family, neighbors, coworkers, and colleagues. Thanks for your continued generosity to provide wisdom and insights. Amen.

THE
EIGHTH LETTER
TO THE KING

LOVING EVERY DAY

Dear Father,

When are you coming to visit this land? It is springtime here, and the land is beautiful. The birds are singing so melodiously that they form a heavenly choir. The beauty of the flowers is incredible after such a long, bitter winter. They are exquisite, so brilliantly and intricately designed.

It is with an upbeat heart that I write you today. The reason for my joy could be spring. However, it could be that I can see your ways at work wherever I turn.

Last night, my husband and I got together with your people again to read and study your letters. What I enjoy about these people is they not only want to read your letters again and again, but they also want to take what they learn and actually change their lives to reflect your teachings.

They enthusiastically spread your message, Father. When I informed them that your most important message for the people of this land is that you love them, you care for them, and you are coming back soon, they all got excited. They can't wait to meet you face to face. This is the longing of their hearts!

However, they have the same struggles I do about how to share your message in a world that doesn't believe you really are king. One person explained that no matter how articulate she is in explaining the facts of your existence and your kingship, many people choose to ignore her words. It's like they are blinded: incapable of seeing; deaf: not able to hear; or stonehearted: unable to feel. This is so sad.

The conclusion we came to is that love is the most powerful tool in proclaiming your message. Love. When we love our families, others will see and believe. When we love our neighbors, they will see and believe. When we love and show kindness and caring to even those who make fun of us, they too will see and believe.

We also discussed the importance of practicing love by asking questions to learn about the other person. We decided that too often we want to talk about the facts of your existence. In reality, all people want to know is that we care. One of the important ways we can show we care is by asking them questions about their dreams, hurts, pains, and frustrations. Listening is an important way to practically show love.

What other suggestions do you have, Father? Oh, yes, I will ask the advisor what his suggestions are also. I haven't done so yet.

In all our time here—most of which I've invested in deepening my relationships with my husband and my children—I still haven't made a choice about where to work and what to do. I wish you were here and would just say, "Do this, Daughter. This job fits you." Even more than that, I wish you would say, "Here, I've created the ideal job for you, my daughter. One that allows you flexibility to be with your family, one that maximizes your skills and talents, one that allows you to build relationships with people so you can proclaim my message, one where you won't get too stressed out, and one that will quickly pay off your debt."

At this point, I don't believe there is a job that can provide all that! Could you surprise me, Father? Could you pull some strings behind the scenes and cause that to happen? Even though that is my desire, Father, I trust your wisdom in choosing me for this task. Your way is the right way. I also know you are magnificent, able to do far beyond what even I can imagine or dream. Help me to trust you even more.

As I mentioned in the beginning, I look forward to your coming visit. I want to hug you forever! My children talk of you often just as they used to. Can we all sit on your lap at one time?

~ Your daughter

MY FATHER'S WORDS

Smiling at the thought of all of us in his lap sharing in his love, I folded the letter, only to look up and see the smiling face of the messenger, ready to take my letter and others to the king. With my gratitude, he started up the path now clearly lined with border stones.

In my heart, I heard my father say, *"My children are those who love. Without this, it is impossible to be my child. I am love. My children give love freely. They are not afraid to be vulnerable, nor do they grieve when the love given is not returned. They are content to know that I return to them much more than they give.*

"Love! Love! Love! That is what the world needs. You have my love, dear children. Share it freely. You cannot run out. The supply is unlimited. The demand is great, but the supply is greater.

"Let the Spirit of holiness guide you into paths of service and love. This is my way for you."

By "love" he did not mean for me to simply feel an emotion. He meant for me to do something to show his love to others.

> **Dear friends, let us love one another,
> for love comes from God.
> Everyone who loves has been born of God
> and knows God.
> Whoever does not love does not know God,
> because God is love.**
>
> 1 John 4:7-8 *(NIV)*

PRACTICAL APPLICATION

Journal your responses, and God's inspired insights, to the following:

Since love is the main tool in proclaiming the Good News of Jesus, then whom has God called you to love?

Since listening is one tangible demonstration of love, who are the people that you might be able to love more completely by listening more deeply?

This love is not merely an emotion; it is an action: *to love.*
What might be some other tangible ways you can show
God's love through actions?

Who are those who are difficult to love? Could it be that
God is developing and forming his character in you through
these difficult people and situations?

Prayer

Dad, how simple you make touching lives for your kingdom:
show love to those who need you! You aren't asking us to simply
speak words on your behalf, but to take action so that others
practically know your love. I ask you to show me meaningful
actions I can do that will have a ripple effect in expanding
your kingdom. If a picture is worth a thousand words, then a
"picture" in motion is worth even more! You are so wise, Father!
Amen.

THE
EIGHTH LETTER
FROM THE KING

KNOWING TRUTH

Dear Daughter,

I received a message from my advisor today, and he informs me that things are getting worse in the land. He talked of all the violence—so much chaos. So many people are getting hurt. If only they would follow my ways.

He also communicated some of the strange beliefs many people follow who do not know me and are not reading my ancient letters. This is what happens when people are left to their own imaginations. They imagine themselves as gods: infinite, all knowing, all wise, and eternal. They talk of great powers they can tap. According to them, all is one—there is no Creator of this land. This is false, and these thoughts will only lead to ruin. This saddens my fatherly heart.

In light of this, Daughter, it is even more important, to remind yourself daily of the truth you have learned from me, and are still learning continually. Truth is a belt that girds you for action. Knowing truth will help you to easily identify the falseness surrounding you. Sometimes the deceit is very insidious and hardly perceptible. Please believe that these subtle lies can distract you from your mission and can bring much sadness and confusion into your life.

I encourage you to talk openly about these matters with my advisor every day. You cannot afford to let anything that is not truth to cloud your thinking. Truth sets you free to be who you were created to be. Truth allows you to see clearly and to stay in close relationship with me. Remember, a heart trained on truth—my word, my provision for salvation, and my will for you—will stay under my protection. A heart living in truth lives abundantly with joy, peace, and strength.

When you find yourself caught up in some untruth, quickly confess. Do not allow an untruth to take root in your life. It will destroy you, my love. Many who espouse these strange ideas are charismatic people, talking about how renewed they are now that they are rid of the old, outdated ideas about me and my kingship. Do not be deceived, my daughter; that feeling of "renewal" is only temporary. It is not lasting peace or lifelong joy. It will fade. You will see.

Embrace the truth. Do not ever let it flee from you.

~ *Father*

MY FATHER'S WORDS

If my father's truth would set me free, then my living that truth would then set others free, would it not? All at once, in my heart, I heard my father say, *"It is possible to misuse the Word I gave you. Do not take a bite here and a bite there. Eat the whole of it.*

"Do not give way to strange ideas. Stay with the ideas I have written and with the leading of your teacher, the advisor. This is my desire for my children. It is the food I have provided. It is good and will meet your needs completely."

Walk? The best way, I mused, was a path that the king's son had long ago established between the villages and the castle. That path would show the king's people the way. I wanted to show them the path.

> **Dear friends, do not believe every spirit,**
> **but test the spirits**
> **to see whether they are from God,**
> **because many false prophets**
> **have gone out into the world.**
>
> **1 John 4:1 (NIV)**

PRACTICAL APPLICATION

Journal your responses, and God's inspired insights, to the following:

What are the practices you have in your life that help you to discern God's truth from this world's falsehood?

What references do you have to help you find God's truth?

How do your spiritual practices and rhythms, which include being in God's Word, living in community with God's people, and praying to the Most High King help in this endeavor?

Consider keeping a journal of possible falsehoods you have uncovered. Contrast those lies with the truths that God's Word reveals as you diligently search Scripture in its full context.

Where do you feel stuck or trapped? Is it possible that there's a falsehood preventing you from experiencing God's goodness and graciousness in that area? What steps can you take to get rid of the false and instill truth?

PRAYER

Dad, I know this world's philosophies can be deceptively enticing, and I won't put myself in danger by denying it. The more I see the stress and confusion those ways bring, the more I want to remain solidly on your path. I need your help to clearly see the falsehoods and to unmistakably hear the subtle deceptions. I trust you to give me strength to instill your truth, so that my life is built on a strong foundation. Amen.

THE
NINTH LETTER
TO THE KING

SUGARCOATED POISON

Dear Father,

Your last letter was very timely. I went to a meeting last night where the speaker kept uttering these seductive ideas . . . suggestions that were half-truths. Ideas that sounded good, but when evaluated against the truth of your kingdom, they were the half-truths you warned me about.

I wanted to be active in identifying what was not 100 percent truthful, so I wrote down the lies or half-truths and compared them with your truth. Here's what I have figured out: In lies and half-truths, the focus is on self. In your truth, the focus is on our relationship with you as our king.

The first lie I identified was that we hold divinity within us.

Your old letters showed that in Adam, we hold death within us. In your Son, we have abundant life through his death and resurrection.

Another half-truth I recognized was that which says we are all expressions of the universe. I see how this can be confusing for some. I know we are all created in your image, but that image becomes marred when we want to do things our own way instead of trusting your way. Once we trust you, your Holy Spirit transforms us so we become expressions of you, our Creator.

Do you know that some people here believe that all the creative energy of the universe wants to manifest itself through us? I find this contradictory to your Word. When we live in alignment with your truth, then your love, life, and light will flow through us to serve others.

It seems strange to me that some people think that humans are unlimited. This is a lie. We are finite beings. Only you are infinite, Father.

One lie that is appealing to those who are not careful is the idea that somehow we can live from the inner place of unlimited freedom, personal power, and joy. Upon closer inspection, I find that without your Son, we are in bondage. There is no deep inner joy. We live in freedom only when we stay closely connected with your advisor, your words (through letters and spoken to our hearts), and your people who love you and are seeking to follow your ways.

Father, some people think the real purpose for us being on Earth is to learn our original state of being. I know this is not true. Our purpose here is to glorify you, our Creator. The only state that allows complete happiness is when we recognize that and then become ambassadors to the world.

When someone said, "The world isn't falling apart because people don't have enough education; it's falling apart because people don't know how to love," I agreed. However, when I look at what those same people think love is, I realize that real, life-changing love comes only from one source—you.

You created humans by hand rather than by spoken word, and then you breathed your life into us. We are distinct from animals in this way. You made us in your image, and joy comes only from the right relationship with you. Some people here believe that throughout evolution, all beings, even animals, have been seeking out happiness. What causes people to believe such things?

I've heard people say that they can choose happiness or sadness. I don't fully agree. Only you can give us real joy and eternal life, Father.

There has been much talk here of abundant life. The problem is that some don't see that abundant life is only available through the life, death, resurrection, and glorification of your Son. They say we need to let go of the fears that keep us from abundant life. It seems like they take your words and turn them around.

Another thing the speaker said last night was that the soul needs eternity every day, so we should stop to smell the roses. As nice as that sounds, what our souls really need is an intimate relationship with you every day. Then when we stop to smell the roses, we can thank you for creating them.

Do you think that if I practice being the person I want to be, it will happen? I think this is another lie. It will fail because we do not have the power to be who we want to be. We want to do good things but end up doing evil. That's why we need a new heart filled with you, Father.

I also heard that if I follow my deep desires, I will find good. This is not truth. The truth is that without you, my deepest desires bring death, not eternal life. I want a new heart that seeks after you.

So many of the ideas that were shared come from doing things on my own, in my own strength. The speaker said we should trust the deep interior of ourselves. He said we could access our intuitive powers and our creative self. The truth is we need to trust you. You are always faithful and lead us in the right direction. We often deceive ourselves. We have to trust you to make us aware of our inner strengths, talents, and creative capabilities. You created us intimately and know us. I don't want to do things on my own. I need you.

The real pearl is not the inner experience. The real pearl is a personal relationship with you.

Why can't they see that inner peace comes only from a relationship with you? That peace comes when we pray without ceasing to the king who loves us beyond measure? They believe, instead, that they can discover peace of mind and become imperturbable to external events that threaten inner peace. They think they can do whatever they need to do to calm their thoughts and create inner security and mastery over their lives. I have found that I can only obtain inner, everlasting security when I rest in you and let you handle my whole life.

Regarding feeling loved and loving others, the speaker last night had things really out of order. He said in order to love others, we just need to act confidently and believe we are loved. This is just more lies. Why "believe" we are loved, when we can *know* we are loved by you? Through the work of your son and the patient work of the advisor, you are transforming us. When we walk with you, we are more than okay; we are daughters of the king!

I'm glad I took notes last night and pondered them, Father, otherwise I might find myself getting sucked into some of those seductive thoughts. I realize there is a spiritual battle raging for my allegiance. However, as your daughter, I will not walk in fear, for I know you are the king and that you are coming back soon.

Thanks for your timely words of wisdom. I'll write more later.

~ *Your loving daughter*

My Father's Words

I could now see that my father had been wise to train me in his loving ways and then send me as an ambassador. The people I met desperately needed him, even though they did not know it or want to admit it. He was also wise to send his advisor with me and to continue his loving instruction through all of his ancient letters and his personal messages to me. I could never do this on my own.

All at once, in my heart, I heard my father say, *"My dear daughter, do you know your good fortune at being able to read my Word? Many of my dear ones are not permitted this joy. Do you use it as you should? My word is to be read and reread. It is to be meditated on by day and by night. When you are doing this, Satan is not able to cause you to fall. You are strong when you are well fed, my daughter.*

"You are aware of the enemy, my sheltered ones. Do not live in fear of him. I am greater than he. Keep your attention fixed on me and on my strength. Go forth to praise and glorify me. That will lead the lost to my path."

Through these continuous whispers, I now felt emboldened by the knowledge of his presence and his might. I *could* be his ambassador, and he would help me through any challenges that would arise.

Suddenly, verses from the ancient Scriptures flooded into my mind, verifying the truth of all that he said.

> *"You are the salt of the earth.*
> *But if the salt loses its saltiness,*
> *how can it be made salty again?*
> *You are the light of the world.*
> *A city on a hill cannot be hidden.*
> *Neither do people light a lamp*
> *and put it under a bowl.*
> *Instead they put it on its stand,*
> *and it gives light to everyone in the house.*
>
> *In the same way, let your light shine before men,*
> *that they may see your good deeds*
> *and praise your Father in heaven."*
>
> **Matthew 5:13a, 14-16 (NIV)**

PRACTICAL APPLICATION

Journal your responses, and God's inspired insights, to the following:

Continue to keep a list of the world's lies you encounter and replace them with God's truth. The insights God leads you to will enable you to grow in effectiveness as an ambassador to the world, and to lovingly explain the difference when seekers ask you. This is a life-long journey.

PRAYER

Dad, everyone on Earth is searching for deeper meaning in their lives, and they're often willing to look anywhere in hopes of answers, except to you. I confess that I may not have been the best ambassador; I have often been filled with judgment, telling people where they are wrong. You ask me to walk close to you so that I radiate your character and your love, joy, peace, patience, kindness, goodness, faithfulness, and gentleness— your Gospel. I need you, Dad. Amen.

THE
NINTH LETTER
FROM THE KING

LIGHTING UP MY LIFE

Dear Daughter,

It was good to hear from you. I am very pleased with you that you took such a wise approach in contrasting the lies with the truth. In a letter to the Romans many years ago, I wrote:

"I can assure you that they are deeply devoted to God; but their devotion is not based on true knowledge. They have not known the way in which God puts people right with himself, and instead, they have tried to set up their own way; and so they did not submit themselves to God's way of putting people right" (Romans 10:2-3, GNT).

That is still true today. In their darkness, they search desperately for light, for meaning. Little do they know that the light they choose is but a flicker compared to my true light. You, my princess, have been sent into this world to be my light and to proclaim where the true light is. Continue your vigilance as you love others and share my life.

You have not talked much of your family lately or of the job you were looking for. What have you decided to do?

I continue with my work that needs to be accomplished before I come to visit. I desire that everyone be given an opportunity to hear my message prior to my return. How is your effort to share my story moving forward, Daughter?

Of course, I have to ask how your conversations with my advisor are going. Have you continued to find him to be as valuable as I told you he would be?

I admire your commitment to meet often with my people for encouragement and to study my letters. Continue in this so you grow even stronger in your ability to walk in my power, purpose, and presence. Walk in confidence. Do not shy away from anyone or anything.

Remember always the rich heritage that is yours, my daughter. My kingdom is yours. Remember that, and do not let your eyes deceive you into bondage in that foreign land.

I love you. I care deeply for you. I am coming back soon. I delight to see you step more fully into your identity as my daughter and your authority as my ambassador.

~ Your father

MY FATHER'S WORDS

Overwhelmed with his love, and confident in his complete confidence in me, I held his letter pressed between both of my hands—my hands were the hands of a king's ambassador, I realized, an ambassador gifted with the ability to touch lives for him. He had chosen the right person when he chose me.

On the road, the messenger passed by, and as always lifted a hand in greeting. I nodded back kindly, contemplating. His hand, I reflected, was that of scars and hard work. It had smoothed rough paths. It had carried our burdens. It had rolled stones to show us the way home.

As he continued on, I realized that many traits about him reminded me of the king. Then I knew. I knew the reason why he maintained the path to the castle. He was the one who had laid them.

He was the son of the king.

In my heart, I heard my father say, *"Dear children, I have given you the keys of the kingdom. Use them to open the doors for others as well as for yourselves. In this I will be well pleased, and Father, Son, and Advisor will be glorified.*

"Great is the love of a father for his children. My love for you is perfect. It passes human understanding and is best demonstrated by Calvary. Has any father done more? It is true that Calvary is the greatest symbol of love, both the Father's and the Son's, but it doesn't stop there. Our love continues. It has no beginning, and no end. Offer your praise for our everlasting love.

"My children serve me willingly. They give without needing to know my complete design. They trust the designing and planning to me. They love my children everywhere. They do not withhold from doing good when they can. They are a pleasure and a joy to me. When I return for my children, the meeting will be one of great joy. Shouts of praise will rend the heavens! I am planning for my own loved ones! Look for my coming. It will not be delayed."

I *would* be the king's ambassador. In so doing, I would give back to him and to others the great love he first gave, and always gives, to me. He did not give me a spirit of timidity, but a spirit of power.

I was a daughter of the king.

> *"But you will receive power*
> *when the Holy Spirit comes on you;*
> *and you will be my witnesses in Jerusalem,*
> *and in all Judea and Samaria,*
> *and to the ends of the earth."*
>
> **Acts 1:8** *(NASB)*

PRACTICAL APPLICATION

Journal your responses, and God's inspired insights, to the following:

Our parable ends in this chapter as the daughter finally—and fully—realizes that she can do all things through God who gives her strength and guidance. She is an ambassador, who is intentional and strategic about nurturing other ambassadors along the journey. Where is God calling you to be a more intentional ambassador? What part of your life might you surrender to him so that you become an ambassador in every part of your life, at home, at work, and in the neighborhood?

How can you intentionally show God's welcoming love to strangers and acquaintances amid simple, everyday tasks? Make a vertical list of your daily activities—where you go and who you typically speak with, even if just exchanging hellos with a grocery store clerk. For example:

- jogging, neighbors
- drive children to school, other parents
- coffee shop, customer service person
- work, coworkers and regular customers

After each, write a few newly inspired ideas of ways you can connect with each one and gradually build a casual friendship with them. Know that each moment has a ripple effect in expanding God's kingdom.

PRAYER

Dad, throughout *Letters from the King* you have answered so many questions I've had regarding how to represent you while being a busy wife and mom. I ask you, as your daughter, to enable the ambassadorship you have instilled in me to be my new habit. When I meet others, may I not judge. Instead may your love radiate through me. Let me be that "someone" for those who need you most. I am your loving daughter, an ambassador to the Most Holy High King. Amen.

Your Father loves you without measure. Show great love in return to God and all your neighbors, near and far.

His Son sacrificed himself to pave a pathway to the Kingdom of heaven. There is no greater act of love. He is your brother, your trusted friend.

The Holy Spirit is your continual advisor. Talk to him, and then listen to his guidance.

Meet often with others strong in the faith. "Though one may be overpowered, two can defend themselves. A cord of three strands is not quickly broken" (Ecclesiastes 4:12).

Be confident. Walk in his authority.

You are an ambassador, an empowered daughter of the king.

AFTERWORD

Dear Reader, Beloved
Daughter of the King,

As a young girl, I experienced a few events that perhaps seem unusual to people who don't believe that God exists, and maybe also to those Christians who haven't had one or two uncommon experiences with God themselves. Does God still do miracles? You know, a better question to ask might be this one: Have *you* experienced a miracle yourself, or has someone you know?

With that thought in mind, permit me to share with you what happened.

When I was six years old, I had what I believed was a God-dream that called me to the mission field as a medical professional. I was certain this dream came from God.

Nine years later, when I was fifteen, I was worshipping the Lord at a Tuesday evening Bible study/prayer meeting (with more than twenty people crammed into a small four-room house). I had a vision that I was in the presence of the glorified Lord. It was unexplainable! I felt unconditionally loved, completely whole, totally pure, and clean. There was no shame, no guilt, and no burden.

While basking in his love, I thought, *Wow! This is so incredible. What can I do to show my love, my devotedness to God?* Not coming up with a good answer, I asked, "Jesus, what would you like me to do for you?"

He replied, "Danita, I have called you to love."

I don't think it was an audible voice. It was a voice that, somehow, I heard at the core of my being.

As an adult, prior to going to medical school, I decided to work for a couple of years to save up money. I interviewed with all kinds of companies and finally came to the decision that there wasn't a single job out there for me. I was a misfit! However, after nine failed interviews, I had one remaining interview with Xerox Corporation.

This time, Frank, the manager, was a hound dog! He was determined to hire me. (He had closed on me what seemed like fifty times prior to this meeting.) Every objection I had to working with Xerox was met with a logical response. The logical answer to this incredible offer from a Fortune 100 company was yes. However, my heart said no, because I knew I was not destined for the business world. I was destined to the mission field, to be a medical missionary.

I left his office with, "Frank, I'm sorry. The last and final answer is no."

As the elevator doors closed behind me on the seventh floor of the Norwest Bank building in downtown Sioux Falls, South Dakota, I heard the Holy Spirit whispering in my heart, "Danita, I have called you to be a missionary . . . a minister in the business world. I want you to say yes."

Again, the voice was one I heard at the core of my being.

I started sobbing. "No, God! I'd rather go to Africa!"

The reply was the same: "I've called you to be a missionary, a minister in the business world."

This was a life-altering event, a dramatic shift of direction. I was so positive of the God-dream I'd had when I was six years old. Yet, the voice was so clear. I was certain it was the Holy Spirit speaking.

I drove home, called Frank, and told him I'd changed my mind and that I would like to accept his offer. In retrospect, I see that God had been preparing me for ministry in the marketplace for quite some time.

In reflecting on this experience, I came to see that God's ways are not my ways! After I heard God's voice, I changed my course of direction. I also learned that God acts. He speaks. He's powerful beyond what we can imagine. In his presence is the love and acceptance that fills our hearts' deepest needs. He has invited us to share his immeasurable, much-needed love: to be his ambassadors.

My hope and prayer for you, my friend, is this:

LOVE. God calls us to love. We often get so caught up in our to-do lists, keep-up-with-the-Joneses lists, and I've-got-my-act-together Super Woman lists, and he keeps bringing us back to *love*. I trust that you come to know his love at the core of your being, so that you constantly overflow with his love to every person you meet and in every situation your encounter.

LIFE. God teaches us daily how to be ambassadors, to be a vessel through which his life-giving Spirit flows. He often prompts us to pray for spouse, children, in-laws, neighbors, clients, employees, and even strangers we see or meet. He also gives us abundant opportunities to encourage, serve, and meet their needs spiritually, relationally, and motivationally. I hope that you increasingly walk with the power, purpose, and presence of the Holy Spirit, overflowing with gratitude and thankfulness for the unlimited riches that are yours in Christ.

LIGHT. If we are called to live a life of 24/7 worship, what does that practically look like in the role of spouse? Parent? Business leader? Colleague? Employer? I challenge you to continuously ask, "How might I lift high the light of Jesus Christ in a practical, down-to-earth way in every situation, whether at home, at work, or in the neighborhood?" I know he will heal and strengthen you as you bring that light to others.

LAUGHTER. When people ask me what advice I have for living, I almost always include, "Hang around people who laugh a lot!" Modern studies show that laughter truly is good medicine for the soul! Plus, we are Christ-followers who know the end of the story. We will be victorious! Laughter is one of the greatest weapons we have to proclaim that God is the victor! So I pray that God empowers you with a deep laughter, and that you are an inspirational joy to those who are searching for his love, life, and light.

LEADERSHIP. It took many years before I began internalizing the truth that God had called me, and is calling me, to leadership. For some reason, I believed a deep-seated, energy-sapping lie that women don't lead. This is my continuing journey. I pray you fully embrace your leadership gifts and talents, presenting them to the King of Kings. He will empower you for kingdom impact.

To be a vessel over-flowing with Love, Life, Light, Laughter, and Leadership, we must walk in the presence, power, and purposes of the Most High King. Therefore, it's important to develop the practices that keep us in tune with what God is doing in us and around us. Continue to develop the spiritual practices of reading the Word, meditating (praying and listening to him), and being involved in a worshipping community. These are important to being fully all that God has designed us to be. These, fellow daughter of the king, enable us to go forth and be his ambassadors of love.

Is a call to love easy to fulfill? No, it isn't. It goes against human nature, and even more, it is a lifelong calling. I've learned that the more clear and distinct God's voice is when he calls us, the more difficult a task might be. That's been true in my life. I've struggled (as someone glued to her to-do lists) to figure out what it means to be a missionary in the professional marketplace, as well as what it means to show love.

It started as a seed God planted in my heart. With his presence and guidance (and constant reminders to love), that seed will continue to grow. With him, all things are possible.

God has called us to love. He is calling you now.

I leave you with this final word:

Fully

Lord,
Help me to fully accept your love,
That I may fully love you with all my heart, soul, mind, and strength.
Help me to fully abide in your Light,
That I may fully shine the Light of Jesus Christ to those around me.
Help me to fully experience your life,
That I may be a full vessel by which your life flows to others.
Help me to fully know your joy and laughter,
That I may fully share your joy and laugh with others.
In the name of Mighty Jesus!
Amen

The meditations, "My Father's Words" are excerpts from My Thoughts Toward You *written by my friend and spiritual mentor, Priscilla. During the writing process, many encouraged me to include all of the meditations. Since these meditations have been such a fresh word of encouragement to me, I wanted to share them with you also.*

MY THOUGHTS TOWARD YOU

by Priscilla Mohrenweiser

Introduction

I was visiting in an isolated village in southwestern Brazil. The Brazilians could not speak my language nor I theirs. Floodwaters kept me there two weeks. That was plenty of time for me to speak to God, and to let him speak to me.

Our conversations continued in other places. The last paragraphs were written in the isolation of my own home during a Minnesota snowstorm.

The psalmist David speaks of "thy thoughts which are to us-ward . . . they are more than can be numbered" (Psalm 40:5 *KJV*). It is my belief that the following thoughts are some of his thoughts which are to us-ward.

May the Holy Spirit within you witness to the truth of them.

~ *Priscilla*

My Thoughts Toward You

My children are those who love. Without this it is impossible
to be my child. I am love. My children give love freely. They are
not afraid to be vulnerable, neither do they grieve when the love
given is not returned. They are content to know that I return to
them much more than they give.

Deut. 7:9, Lk. 10:27, Eph. 5:1-2, 1 Jn. 3:1

My desire for communication with my children is not satisfied
by a brief word from them daily. I want to reveal my love to
them. I want to share my desires and my plans with them, and I
want to hear them as they offer sweet sacrifices of praise to me.
This takes time, but it is time redeemed. Don't be afraid to give
me your best hours. They will be blessed and all the hours of the
day will become exceedingly precious in my presence.

Ps. 28:7, Ps. 32:8, Jer. 29:11, Phil. 4:6

Love! Love! Love! That's what the world needs. You have my
love, dear children. Share it freely. You cannot run out. The
supply is unlimited. The demand is great, but the supply is
greater. How I long to encircle the world with my arms of love. I
must do it through you now.

Jn. 13:34-35; 17:21, Rom. 12:10

My children give me joy when they are concerned about
my family everywhere. They please me when they are
compassionate and are willing when it lies within their power,
to alleviate suffering. They please me greatly when my concerns

become their concerns, and thus they share in my sufferings. Then my heart rejoices because together we are sharing the work of my Kingdom. Those who do this will one day be prepared to reign with me.

Prov. 19:17, Is. 58:6–11, 1 Jn. 4:7-8

It is possible to misuse the Word I gave you. Do not take a bite here, and a bite there. Eat the whole of it, sometimes in big bites, other times in small pieces. Balance one section with another. Do not give way to strange ideas. Stay with the main ideas and the leading of your teacher, the Holy Spirit. This is my desire for my children. It is the food I have provided. It is good and will meet your needs completely. Your food is ready! Come and eat!

Deut. 8:3, Jer. 15:16, Matt. 4:4, Rom. 16:17

I want to teach you many things, my children, but your minds are filled with the thoughts and rules of this present world. Give me both your hearts and your minds. I need both places to guide you into the paths of goodness and righteousness. In this, your way will be filled with Light. You will know real wisdom, which is from above and is pure.

Ps. 111:10, Prov. 1:5, Phil. 4: 8-9

My children are those who constantly delight me by their obedience. They care not that others walk differently. They are pleased only when they know they are in my place for them. This place may be the same place as they were in last year, or twenty years ago. It is a place of joy for them because they know that they are abiding in me, and I am leading them moment by moment. My perfect plan may not seem spectacular, but it is good because it is my plan.

Sam. 15:22, Ps. 23, Phil. 4:11-12, Jn. 15:4

Children of Mine are priceless. They are worth more than the whole world to Me. I am exceedingly pleased when new children are born into My Kingdom. There is no pleasure greater than this for Me. Children of Mine, tell others about My Kingdom of love.

Darkness surrounds you, children of Light. Shine in all your goodness. Shine in love. Let the world see me again.

Ps. 89:15, Jn. 1:1-4, Eph. 5:7-9

Children of the harvest fields, this is the time to work quickly. Give yourself to harvesting while the grain is ripe and ready. There will be a long time to rest when the harvest is over. I have chosen you to share in this work of mine. I will enable you to continue until the harvest for you is completed.

Lk. 10:2, Matt. 11:28-30, Gal. 6:9

This is a day for rejoicing in my presence, for praising my goodness, for giving attendance to my Word. Rejoice in such an opportunity and use it to its best advantage. This will prepare you for the day when you praise and rejoice eternally.

Do you have fears that tomorrow will be cloudy and dark? Do you not know that when I am with you this darkness becomes light? This is my word for you, children. I am with you and will keep you in all places.

Ps. 13:5, Ps. 27:1, Phil. 4:4, 2 Tim. 3:16-17

When it appears that you are not accomplishing great things, remember that my thoughts of great things are different from yours. My thoughts include obedience in small things as well as great. Rewards are not given according to greatness of deeds, but according to obedience and love. The last will be first—do you not remember, my loved ones?

Micah 6:8, Matt. 20:16, Mk. 9:41, Lk. 16:10

Children of mine have security. Satan cannot give hope, neither here nor in the world to come. He can give pleasure for a moment, but such pleasure passes quickly, and how empty are the hours that follow. Children of mine have pleasure here, and promise of joy unspeakable in the world to come. Oh my beloved, follow me with joy and obedience. This is the beginning of joy in my presence.

Ps. 119:165, Jn. 10:28, Eph. 1:3-14

My beloved ones may rest in peace when all else is troubled. I give peace that originates in the heart; therefore it is protected from outward disturbances. My children may have an abundance of peace in every situation. Trust me completely. In this lies your peace.

Is. 54:10, Jn. 14:27, Eph. 3:20

My youngest children are as precious to me as my oldest children. Age makes no difference to me. I love the little ones in their helplessness. I love those who have the fervency of youth, and I love those who have the mellowness that comes from maturity. Each is equally precious as my child.

Prov. 16:31, Matt. 18:2-6, Gal. 3:26

Children of mine are so precious to me that I will permit nothing to touch them that I have not ordained. My children can rest secure in my love and all-knowing care. My perfect knowledge keeps me from error. Trust me to guide and provide perfectly for you.

Ps. 37:23-24, Matt. 6:31-32, Phil. 4:19, 1 Jn. 5:14-15

My children do not always receive kind treatment from the children of this present world. This is to be expected, and accepted with joy. But I am grieved beyond words when my children are not kind to one another. Not only does it grieve me but it impedes the work of my Kingdom. Children, love one another.

Prov. 25:21, 2 Cor. 13:11, Eph. 4:32, 1 Jn. 4:20

How often my children feel lonely and forsaken. It is not so! I never leave nor forsake. I permit their faith to be tried that it may become as refined gold, but nothing touches them which is unknown by me. Children of this lonely world, remember you are really citizens of another world, and there is no loneliness there.

Deut. 31:8, Phil. 3:20, 1 Pet. 1:7

Children of this present world, the difficulties are great for you. Doubts and discouragements come to you. The entrance of many false doctrines gives rise to much darkness in this world. Look to me, not to the darkness. In the light of my countenance, you will find peace and rest.

We encourage women around the
world to realize their value and reach
their potential through job training
and education. As a result, many now
own a business and feed and care
for their own children.

Seventy-six women have graduated
from our Women's Empowerment
Initiative in Tanzania and have
averaged a 47% increase in income
through their small businesses.

*Proceeds of this book directly benefit
the participants of our Tanzanian
Women's Empowerment Initiative.*

For more information, please visit
convoyofhope.org/we

HOPE
FOR
EVERY
WOMAN

Continually have faith in my goodness. I cannot repeat this often enough. My children, rest in me, trust me, and be not afraid.

Ps. 23, Jn. 16:33, Js. 1:2-4

My knowledge of each of my children is perfect. I put each one in the place that is best suited to him. I do not put goats in green pastures and cattle on rocky mountainsides. The plan I have for each child will be revealed to him step by step. In the time to come you will see the total perfection of my plan.

Prov. 3:5-6, Is. 43:18-19, Rom. 8:28-29

My children, have the clouds overshadowed the sun? Know this: the sun is still there, giving light and warmth. Have the clouds of doubt and darkness hid the Son? Know that he is still there. His warmth and light reach you through the clouds, but one day the clouds will move and you will again walk in the brilliance of his unclouded presence.

Deut. 4:29, 2 Sam. 23:4, Jn. 16:33

When the opportunity to do good to one another is upon you, move! Do not hesitate! Satan laughs when you withhold good from one another. The greatest thing in the world is love. This Satan is unable to produce. My children, walk in love toward one another.

Is. 1:17, Matt. 25:40, Phil. 2:3-7

Children of mine are exceedingly precious to me. I cannot bear to see them suffer unnecessarily. I will heal in body and in spirit. Trust me to make you well and whole in all ways.

Children of mine need have no fear of the future. My greatest desire is to have them here with me. My eagerness to have them with me surpasses any desire they have to be here.

Lk. 4:18-19, 2 Cor. 1:3-4, 2 Tim. 1:12

Today is the day for which you must give account. Take it and offer each moment to me in faith. I will accept such offerings and sanctify each second. In the very ordinary activities, I will bless the work of your hands. In the activities that require special guidance, I will lead. In all things I will be glorified. My children, come to me in love, not fear. My desires for this day, and all others, are that you may increase in wisdom and knowledge, and find favor with me and with your fellow travelers.

Again, my children, give me much praise. There is no way to please me more than to exhibit a heart full of genuine praise. To praise shows a heart that is trusting me. This is my greatest need—to have you trust me. Praise and trust go hand in hand. Both things are precious in my sight.

Ps. 56:4, Prov. 16:3, 1 Cor.10:31, Col. 3:23, 1 Thess. 5:16-18

My beloved sons and daughters in all parts of the world will join in praising me forever. This is my reason for desiring them to live in love and praise now. I will give them mighty songs of love and adoration here if they will listen to me. My children please me most when they live in love and praise.

Ps. 66:4, Eph. 5:2

I am able to bring good out of what seems bad. My dear ones, commit the troublesome things to me. These can be made to work for you, not against you. Satan cannot touch that which I have sanctified.

My dear ones have only to ask and I deliver. They have only to request and I respond. Continue to lay your requests before me. My goodness fails not.

Prov. 3:6, 1Pet. 5:7

Many things in this present world are good. I created them perfectly. My beloved ones, enjoy these things as gifts from me and rejoice in my goodness and perfection in creation.

Dearest friends of mine are those whose hearts are set to do my will. Their actions may not be perfect but it is the set of their desires and wills that is dear to my heart.

Deut. 4:29, Ps. 148:7-10, Matt. 6:33, Col. 1:16

It is interesting that often my children do not recognize my gifts. They fight against the very thing I am sending them. This should not be. In complete trust accept all that comes as having been judged by me and permitted for some purpose. This will please me and make it possible to accomplish my purpose quickly and without difficulty.

Deut. 28:2-6, 1 Thess. 5:18, Js. 1:17

All things were created with the enjoyment of mankind in mind. Therefore, do not despise any of my creatures or creations. Treat all with respect and compassion. In the original plan all things were perfect. It is not so now, but this is my concern, not yours. One day all will be perfect again, and you will understand my grief when my creatures or creations are mistreated. My children, treat all that comes into your lives as if it were from me.

Neh. 9:6, Job 12:7-10, Rev. 4:11

My children delight me when they wait on me continually, asking for my wisdom and my way. What a joy it is to have children who desire to please me more than anything else! They shall have the desires of their hearts.

My children cause me to be filled with joy when they listen to my Word and obey. Obedient children make a father's heart rejoice and be at peace.

Is. 40:31, Jer. 7:23, Js. 1:22, 2 Jn. 1:6

When I find it necessary to discipline my children, I do it in love and not in anger. My soul is deeply grieved when they must be disciplined. I would that they would walk with me in obedience. It is better and more pleasant to teach in that manner.

Deut. 28: 1-14, Prov. 3:12, 1 Cor. 11:32

You are aware of the enemy, my sheltered ones. Do not live in fear of him. I am greater than he. Keep your attention fixed on me and on my strength, and go forth to praise and glorify me.

My children give me joy when they withhold nothing from me, when nothing is more important than obeying me. I will give priceless blessings to those who walk with me in this manner.

Deut. 6:18, Ps. 91:9-10, 1 Jn. 4:4

Dearest children of mine are listening children. They hear me, recognize my voice, and respond. When I come in splendor and glory, their ears will be attuned to the sound of my arrival. They will live in my presence forevermore and will not need my voice of guidance. They will stay with me and judge those who listened not. Be diligent in waiting on me and in listening for the sound of my voice. It comes in the language of love.

Is. 55:3, Prov. 2:1-5, Jn. 10:27

Many times I must permit my children to suffer in one manner or another. It is not possible to get pure gold without fire, and it is not possible to get purified lives without suffering. Do not think the suffering will harm you; it will cause you to shine more brilliantly for me.

Zech. 13:9, 1 Pet. 1:7, Js. 1:2-4

Dear children, I have given you the keys of the Kingdom. Use them to open the doors for others as well as for yourself. In this I will be well pleased and my Father will be glorified.

Great is the love of a father for his children. My love for you, my children, is perfect. It passes human understanding, and is best demonstrated by Calvary. Has any father done more?

Ps. 103:13, Matt. 16:19, Gal. 6:2, Eph. 2:10

Beloved children are guided well and watched closely. My eye is that of a loving parent. All signs of growth in wisdom and knowledge and love cause me to rejoice. Those things in your life which impede perfect growth cause me to grieve. Search your hearts and lives. Throw out what puts barriers between us. Invite the Holy Spirit to teach you how to follow me more perfectly. This is his job. He will give you all that you need. He will teach and console and help you.

Ps. 139:23-24, Jn. 14:26, 2 Pet. 3:18

My dear children, do you know your good fortune at being able to read my Word? Many of my children struggle to be like me, but are not able to read what I have written for them. Others of my dear ones are not permitted this joy. Do you use it as you should?

Meditate on my goodness. Your faith will increase, and you will be happy, rejoicing children of mine. The world will be attracted by your peace and your joy.

Ps. 104:34, 2 Tim. 3:16, 1 Jn. 1:7

The story of love is best told by your life. The song of songs is best sung by your manner of living. This tremendous truth of my provision for salvation is best demonstrated by your brokenness over Calvary.

This day is a gift, as are all days. Rejoice and give thanks, my children, for the wonderful plan I have for you, and for the wonderful plan by which the worlds exist. I am the Maker of heaven and Earth.

Ps. 118:24, Mic. 6:8, Jn. 13:34-35, Eph. 1:3, 2 Tim. 1:9

Has it seemed long—the waiting for my return? Occupy yourselves, my children, in doing my works and the will of him who sent me. Then the time will pass quickly, and you will be abundantly prepared for my soon return.

Can you be a servant and not serve? Can you be my child and not love? Let the Spirit of holiness guide you into paths of service and love. This is my way for you, children of the harvest fields.

Is. 43:10, Jn. 12:26, Rom. 12:9-13, 2 Pet. 3:14

These days of approaching sorrow and increasing wickedness signal also my approaching return. Be content to fix your mind on my return, not on the darkness of sin which abounds. It is always true that you must think about things that are lovely, and true, and of good report.

Prayer is not a monologue. It is listening as well as talking. Wait quietly before me. You will hear me.

Ps. 27:14, Phil. 4:8, 2 Tim. 3:1-5

Be at peace with those of your own household. If you cannot do this, do not think that you can get along well in the household of God. Give place constantly to those around you. Take the place of humility. Do the work of a servant willingly. You are my children, and I was a servant to all.

Lev. 19:17-18, Mk. 10:45, Eph. 4:1-3, 1 Tim. 3:5

We have many enemies of our Kingdom, children. They do not love me. They love darkness more than light, nighttime more than day, evil more than good. It is not strange that it should be so. You are children of the day. Walk as children of the Light, willing to have all you do made known. One day it will be, you know.

Ps. 37:17, Lk. 8:17, 1 Jn. 1:7

My Kingdom cannot be explained in your language, my
dear ones, just as a father cannot explain things of maturity
to a newborn or young child. Therefore, I can only give you
a glimpse of my Kingdom. The greatest thing there cannot
be imagined by you. It will be wonderful beyond your finest
dreams. One glimpse of it would make your desire to be there
insatiable.

1 Cor. 2:9; 13:12

The time is coming when I will no longer speak words of love
and peace. I will speak words of judgment. I have not come to
condemn, but condemnation comes from refusal to accept my
love. Encourage people everywhere to accept all that I have for
them. You yourselves must be examples of this, my dear ones.
You cannot teach well what you do not do well.

Gen. 12:2, Matt. 28:19, 1 Pet. 4:17, 2 Pet. 3:11-14

This period of waiting has its purposes, although they may not
be visible to you. My children, trusting me completely, must
accept such periods of time and use them to the best advantage
possible. Waiting does not mean just sitting. Continue to do
your work well where you are. Then you will be ready to move
into your new situation, knowing that you have previously done
your best.

Ps. 37:7-8, Jn. 15:4-5, Col. 3:23-24

How beautiful are the feet of those who bring good news in
the far and distant places of the world! I will be their constant
companion. My presence and guidance will be wonderfully real

because they cannot look to others for their guidance and their help. Children of the wilderness places, the desert, too, is mine. I will bring forth roses out of dry and barren ground when you permit the rivers of living water to flow through you. I am the God of the impossible. It is my joy to do for you what others cannot do. Trust me. In my time fruit will be borne.

My children need to have merry hearts. This joy that is infectious is my good gift to those who are wholly trusting in me. It is not difficult to rejoice when you have all you need. I have promised to supply this for you. Therefore rejoice! Sing for joy! Laugh and love!

Is. 52:7, Hab. 3:17-18, Josh. 1:9, Lk. 1:37, Phil. 4:4-7

Holidays are good and necessary. They provide for you necessary changes from routine. My children, enjoy the good things that I have provided, but always in the light of my countenance, and in the joy of my presence.

My Word is to be read and reread. It is to be meditated on by day and by night. When you are doing this, Satan is not able to cause you to fall. You're strong when you are well fed, my children. Eat well!

Josh. 1:9, Ps. 116:7, Matt. 4:4, Mk. 6:31

Has the power of darkness misled you? Do not continue in his way. Return to the paths of goodness and mercy. Do you remember with what joy the father received the prodigal son? Will I do less? Come, bow down and worship. Fall at my feet in confession of sin. I will welcome you with open arms. Together we will feast and rejoice in our reunion.

Is. 44:22, Eph. 6:11, Rev. 2:5

My love is everlasting. It does not waver. Do not permit the enemy to discourage you. I do not turn from you when you fail, children most dear. I wait for you to come to me for forgiveness and cleansing. I have arms open wide to sinners. Cleansing is a most wonderful experience, my children, do not live in filth when the cleansing fountain is available. Live and walk as children of purity and cleanness.

Ps. 51:7, Jas. 5:16, 1 Jn. 1:9

Children in a valley of shadows, the sun is still shining! You may not see it, you may not even feel its warmth, but it is still there. When the shadows surround you, rest in the assurance that my love is from everlasting to everlasting. It does not change. Count on this and be at peace.

Is. 42:16, Jn. 16:33, Rom. 8:38-39

When I return for my children, the meeting will be one of great joy. Shouts of praise will rend the heavens! What a day of rejoicing I am planning for my own loved ones! Look for my coming. It will not be delayed.

This day of trouble will pass for you, my children. It is only a brief time. Think of others for whom total darkness is just beginning. Bring them to the Light that overcomes darkness.

Is. 51: 11-13, Matt. 24:42, Rev. 22:12

It seems that others receive more praise for service rendered. Does this bother you? I have said that much praise given here may be the only praise received. But when works of love go unnoticed by your fellow man, I never fail to see this and plan for future rewards. My children, learn to think in my terms. Permit me to guide your minds and thoughts by my Spirit. This is what is meant by the renewing of your minds.

Jn. 14:26, Rom. 12:1-2, Heb. 6:10

Christmas is a time of celebration commemorating my first coming. Easter recalls my death and resurrection. But for you Pentecost ought to be celebrated also. The gift of my Spirit is the greatest thing I have done for you after providing salvation. Don't miss the importance of this.

Is. 11:2, Lk. 4:8, Acts 2:1-4

The Holy Spirit gives you glimpses of your unworthiness and my righteousness. He reveals my glory. He does not draw attention to himself. My children, the Holy Spirit is my best gift to you. Would you live without the best gift I can give? This gift of love is waiting for you. He will renew your mind and open the windows of your understanding. He gives guidance as I instruct. He is your only source of assistance in understanding my Word. Invite him into your life.

Jn. 14:16-17; 16:13, Rev. 4:4

When the Comforter has come to make his home in you, you will know power in your life. You will be amazed at the simple way he blesses and gives guidance. He never distracts from my glory. Children of mine, don't miss my greatest helper for you. Don't walk in weakness when you can walk in power.

Lk. 24:49, 1 Cor. 6:19-20, Eph. 4:30

There are no creatures of my creation that do not struggle to gain the necessities of life. All must do this. It is my plan for creatures great and small. The struggle may differ from the polar bear to the ant, and from the ostrich to the hummingbird, but each works to gain the necessary food and drink. My children, too, must work to gain the necessities of life. It is not good that others provide what you should labor for. If you have more than is necessary, thank me, and give to those who are weak or sick or unable to work. In so doing, the plan for your existence is accomplished and has purpose. Despise not hard labor nor long hours of toil. By this also I am glorified.

Ps. 128:2, Prov. 30:25

This time of sorrow will pass, too. It is not possible for my children to live only in the shadows. I provide sun and light as it is needed. I know your needs and will supply accordingly. I desire greatly to have healthy, normal children. For this reason you must have both sun and shade. The shade or shadows may simply be a resting place for you. Accept it as such. The sun will surely shine again.

Ps. 91:1; 113:3; Phil. 4:19

When I planned for my people to celebrate my death and resurrection by partaking of my body and blood, I planned perfectly. Don't refuse my invitation to partake of it. Don't speak lightly of such an occasion. Don't treat lightly my best gifts. I grieve deeply over carelessness in this sharing of my body and my blood. It is the result of unbelief that makes you act so. If you believed me you would attend to this with great reverence.

Lk. 22:19-20, 1 Cor. 10:16-17; 11:28

The children of the enemy have many problems. It may not seem so, but it is true. They have many problems, but they have no counselor or comforter. You have both, my dear ones. This should be a source of strength and stability for you. Would you not rather be in my family, though there are often hardships? Along with hardship there is hope for all who trust in me.

Ps. 25:1-2, Col. 1:9-13, Jas. 1:12

My children, do not define for others their calling or their work. Permit me to guide my own beloved ones. You may encourage, confirm, or give question, but you may not give direction without my direction being given first. Trust me to guide my children aright.

Children of the day, again I say to you—be at peace. The sign of your walking in my presence will be that peace rules in your life. No one can deny my presence in a life that exhibits peace.

The truth of trusting me to give guidance directly to the person involved cannot be underplayed. It is important that I be able to freely guide each of my own children. By this, I will be able to accomplish my most desired ambitions for them. They will be in my place for them. They will hear my voice, and they will become mature.

Ps. 16:11, Prov. 3:6, Eph. 4:1-3

This sacrifice of praise that you offer is not without effort. Sometimes it is very difficult. It pleases me greatly when my children praise me when they do not feel like it, when they are not experiencing miracles, only drudgery and hard work. This kind of praise must come from a heart that has confidence in my good providence, and doubts not my judgment of what is best.

Ps. 34:1, Ps. 150, Heb. 13:15, 1 Pet. 4:16

Angels have many uses in my Kingdom. How often I have used them to comfort the weary! I myself was comforted by them after temptation, and in the Garden of Gethsemane. Children of mine, angels are one more provision of mine for your welfare and good. My angels have charge over you, lest you stumble and be unable to rise.

Ps. 34:7; 91:11, Heb. 13:2

My angel of death is often thought bad. He is not bad. He is my faithful servant. He will call you one day. He will touch you. Do not live in fear of this servant of mine. He will bring you into my presence and to eternal joy. Children of mine, I am eager to have you in my presence. Let me set your affections in this direction.

Ecc. 3:1-2, Jn. 14:27, Phil. 1:21-23

Satan has his armies. They are like him. They have no love. They must bow before my power. Don't permit them any place in your life. Even here, you have the power to reign. My blood and righteousness permit you to do this. Don't trust in yourself. Plead my promises and my blood. Satan and his angels will be defeated. Darkness will be overcome by Light.

Matt. 19:26, Rom. 16:20, Jas. 4:7

My children are those who love freely—when it is returned and when it is not. I put within them a fountain which gives forth love and praise. When they are walking in the light of my countenance, the fountain overflows, and its contents spill out to others. It is rich in life-giving properties. It will be the place where many begin to desire to have such a fountain themselves.

Matt. 5:13-16, Lk. 11:33, Jn. 4:14

Children of mine give me joy when they wait patiently for my answers, when they do not give way to discouragement at delayed responses. I will surely answer in due season and will give more than they ask or think. Because they trust me, much shall be entrusted to them. They will be rich in wealth that lasts forever.

Ps. 38:15, Eph. 3:20, 2 Pet. 3:8-9

When I come again to the Earth—when the trumpet sounds and those who have died rise—you, my children, will experience the greatest thrill it is possible to experience. Your faith will become reality. That which you believed will be true. You will not regret for one minute the long wait, nor the doubts and fears. I will be to you much more than I have promised.

Children, be ready and waiting. My coming draws nigh!

In the twinkling of an eye it shall be accomplished. There will be no time for preparation then, no time to invite others. Do today what you would do if I should appear this day.

Dear children, to have faith is to trust in the unseen forces that govern this Earth. It is to see beyond the concrete to the visionary. It is to look at darkness and see my Light. It is to look at sickness and see my health. It is to look at this world and see the next one.

Matt. 25:1-13, 1 Cor. 15:52, Heb. 11:1-2

My children believe in miracles, for they themselves are miracles. Their lives show forth resurrection power. They have seen the work of my hands and believe that I am all power. They stagger not at the impossible. They trust me to do what no one else can do.

It is true that Calvary is the greatest symbol of my love, and of the Father's love, but it doesn't stop there. Our love continues. It has no beginning, and no end. Offer your praise for our everlasting love.

Jn. 14:12, 15:13; Acts 3:6, Phil. 2:13

Have you desired something in prayer? Have you asked and not received? Think not that your desire is unknown to me. Think rather that my knowledge permits me to choose the best time for the answer. It is not always my best for you to receive a prompt answer. Trust me to send the right answer at the right time. What may seem like a long delay to you may be just momentary to me.

Ps. 40:1, Rom. 5:4; 8:25

My children love to see my work progress. They do not withhold deserved praise from other believers. They comfort, exhort, and love without measuring the results. My best aims for them are realized in their encouragement of one another. They do not make sport of one another. Their actions are controlled by love.

Mk. 12:31, Rom. 15:1, 1 Thess. 5:11

This is a time for giving thanks. Asking is for other times. Today praise me for all that I have done for you. There will not be time for other things if you do this. It will rise as a sweet sacrifice to me, my children.

My children serve me willingly. They give without needing to know my complete design. They trust the designing and planning to me. They love my children everywhere. They do not withhold from doing good when they can. They are a pleasure and a joy to me.

Ps. 100:4, Prov. 17:22, Gal. 6:9, Col. 3:17

Your life in me is a growing experience. Do not be discouraged when you make mistakes. It's your heart attitude that matters to me. I expect that my children will have to learn many things by experimentation. All children learn step by step. You will avoid many mistakes by listening carefully to me. However, some things are learned only through experience. Through failure you are kept humble and useful. Let failure be just another vehicle in perfecting my image within you.

Ps. 37:24, 2 Cor. 12:9, 1 Jn. 1:8-10

My beloved children rejoice in spending time in my presence. Conversation and fellowship between an earthly father and his children can be exceedingly sweet. Conversation and fellowship between me and my children can be like heaven itself. I have not called you servants only. I have called you friends.

Ps. 19:14, Matt. 6:9-10, Jn. 15:15, 1 Jn. 3

When my children are instant in prayer, I am instant in attention. It is not always best for them that I answer instantly, but they have my attention and my guidance.

My children, your past need not trouble you. As far as the east is from the west—that far have I removed your transgressions from you. In my sight you are righteous. Walk in that knowledge.

Ps. 103:12, Is. 61:10, Phil. 4:19, Rev. 3:20

Has darkness overwhelmed you, dear ones? Come again to the Light. Do not continue to be occupied with the things of this world and the attractions which are momentary. Again, give your attention to the things which are eternal. They will not slip out of your hands and disappear. They become more and more certain day by day.

Ps. 37:7-8, Eph. 5:7-8, Col. 3:2

This isn't the time for sleeping. The night is approaching, but continue to work while you can. The rest will be even more wonderful for those who have labored long and hard. You will rest in my presence and rejoice in my Kingdom forevermore. Children of mine delight me when they are constantly looking for ways to follow me more closely, to please me more completely. For such children, my way is one of joy and peace. For rebellious children, the way becomes hard and frustrating. Choose the best way.

Jer. 32:41, Matt. 24:42, Col. 3:1-4

My children, I have shared much of my love and of my concerns
for you. Now I would have you search my Word. Live in it daily.
The time has come for you to put it into your hearts where no
man can take it from you. The Holy Scriptures are your center of
learning. The Holy Spirit is your teacher. As you live in the Word
you will become wise concerning the things of my Kingdom,
and will learn more and more about my Father and about me.
Peace! My children, Peace!

Jn. 14:26, Heb. 4:12, 1 Thess. 2:13

ABOUT THE AUTHORS

Danita Bye

With a master's degree in Transformational Leadership from Bethel University, Danita is a catalyst for inspiring others to a more active faith, having been called to minister to the business world (while standing alone in an elevator).

"Danita is a God-loving, fresh thinking, encouragement-filled breath of fresh air."

—*Reverend Rick Mylander, Omaha, Nebraska*

Since the motivating elevator chat with God, Danita has become a successful businesswoman in both the corporate and entrepreneurial sectors. She is the founder and CEO of Sales Growth Specialists and The Center for Marketplace Ministers. She is currently launching a new initiative, World-Changers.

Danita is an inspiring, sought-after speaker and long-standing member of the National Speakers Association. She's been a guest speaker at Bethel University, St. Catherine University, the University of St. Thomas Center for Entrepreneurship, and the University of Minnesota's Carlson School of Management, as well as in many corporate environments.

She is the author of eight books and more than fifty articles, which teach and inspire professionals to achieve unmatched success in leadership, sales, and management. In 2005, Danita was named one of 25 Women to Watch by the Twin Cities' (Minneapolis, St. Paul) *Business Journal*. In 2006, she was heralded as the 2006 Woman on the Way by the National Association of Women Business Owners (NAWBO). In 2010, she was named a Power Player by *Minnesota Business* magazine.

A woman of rural beginnings, Danita, the oldest of four, grew up in Cowboy Country, a large, scenic cattle ranch in an isolated part of northwestern North Dakota. In junior high, cattle prices went up, so the family moved from an 800-square-foot, four-room house (with no running water!) to a place that had running water. And no outhouse. And a real bathtub. During these formative years, she learned the value of the dollar, relationships, discipline, education, and faith. Today, those values form the foundation of who she is. Danita has been married for twenty-seven years and has three children.

To learn more about how Danita can help your business, visit www.SalesGrowthSpecialists.com. To ask Danita to speak at your church or Christian event, visit www.Marketplace-Ministers.com.

Priscilla Mohrenweiser

Formerly an elementary school teacher in St. Cloud, Minnesota, Priscilla penned the *My Father's Words* meditations more than thirty-five years ago. Priscilla wrote, photocopied, bound them into book form as *My Thoughts Toward You*, and then gave the books out as gifts.

An educator of adults, Priscilla has taught extensively about prayer—specifically, *listening* to God's reply—and has led countless pastors and their congregations to greater faith walks with God.

Now retired, Priscilla lives at the Covenant Village Retirement Community in Minneapolis, Minnesota, where she inspires and leads elderly people to pray for those in need of God's love and special care, while also reminding those pray-ers how much they still can do to make a difference in the lives of others, and how very much they still matter.